Vedic Astrology

Astrology

The Origins and Core Concepts of Jyotish

(A Complete Guide to Vedic Astrology, From the Perspective of Nakshatras)

Devon Bouck

Published By **Tyson Maxwell**

Devon Bouck

All Rights Reserved

Vedic Astrology: The Origins and Core Concepts of Jyotish (A Complete Guide to Vedic Astrology, From the Perspective of Nakshatras)

ISBN 978-1-7775767-2-1

No part of this guidebook shall be reproduced in any form without permission in writing from the publisher except in the case of brief quotations embodied in critical articles or reviews.

Legal & Disclaimer

The information contained in this book is not designed to replace or take the place of any form of medicine or professional medical advice. The information in this book has been provided for educational & entertainment purposes only.

The information contained in this book has been compiled from sources deemed reliable, and it is accurate to the best of the Author's knowledge; however, the Author cannot guarantee its accuracy and validity and cannot be held liable for any errors or omissions. Changes are periodically made to this book. You must consult your doctor or get professional medical advice before using any of the suggested remedies, techniques, or information in this book.

Upon using the information contained in this book, you agree to hold harmless the Author from and against any damages, costs, and expenses, including any legal fees potentially resulting from the application of any of the information provided by this guide. This disclaimer applies to any damages or injury caused by the use and application, whether directly or indirectly, of any advice or information presented, whether for breach of contract, tort, negligence, personal injury, criminal intent, or under any other cause of action.

You agree to accept all risks of using the information presented inside this book. You need to consult a professional medical practitioner in order to ensure you are both able and healthy enough to participate in this program.

Table Of Contents

Chapter 1: Vedic Astrology And Finance Understanding Vedic Astrology................ 1

Chapter 2: Basics Of Vedic Astrology 7

Chapter 3: Principles Of Financial Prosperity In Vedic Astrology 14

Chapter 4: Analyzing The Birth Chart For Financial Success..................................... 20

Chapter 5: Planetary Influences On Financial Prosperity The Role Of Jupiter In Wealth Accumulation 26

Chapter 6: Identifying Favorable Time Periods For Financial Growth 33

Chapter 7: Remedies And Practices For Enhancing Financial Prosperity 39

Chapter 8: Case Studies And Examples Of Financial Success Using Vedic Astrology 45

Chapter 9: Integrating Vedic Astrology And Financial Planning 58

Chapter 10: Vedic Astrology The Core.... 65

Chapter 11: The Differences Between Vedic As Well As Western Astrology 69

Chapter 12: Zodiac Significations In Astrology.................................. 77

Chapter 13: Planets In Astrology 112

Chapter 14: Houses In Astrology 145

Chapter 16: Yogas 178

Chapter 1: Vedic Astrology And Finance
Understanding Vedic Astrology

Vedic Astrology also referred to as Jyotish and Jyotish, is an ancient Indian method of astrology which has been used since the beginning of time. It's founded upon the notion that the motions and positions of celestial bodies influence the lives of people and provide useful insights into many aspects of life, like financial wealth.

In this chapter in this chapter, we'll explore the mysterious universe that is Vedic Astrology and discover how you can use it to improve financial wellbeing. If you're a novice or already have a basic understanding of astrology This chapter will provide the reader with a thorough knowledge of the concepts and methods employed in Vedic Astrology to make financial predictions.

One of the main ideas that is a part of the Vedic Astrology is the notion of "dashas" or planetary periods. Dashas are the way to divide a person's time into distinct time intervals governed by different planets. When analyzing the system of dashas, Vedic astrologers can predict favorable or unfavorable times to ensure stability and financial growth. Knowing the dasha system will aid you in making informed choices on career and investment choices and financial strategy.

A further important part that is integral to the Vedic Astrology is the study of the chart for birth, also known as "kundli." Birth charts are a distinct diagram of the locations of celestial bodies during the time the individual's birth. It can provide valuable information about the personality of an individual, their strengths, weaknesses and possible financial opportunities. When analyzing a charts of birth, Vedic Astrologers are able to identify advantageous planetary pairings that will help in successful financial growth and assist individuals toward the most suitable path for their career as well as investment opportunities.

Furthermore there is the fact that Vedic Astrology employs a variety of predictive methods like planetary transits, aspects and yogas to provide an overall insight into one's financial future. These methods help to identify the most the most favorable times for accumulating wealth or business ventures as well as the financial investment.

Knowing the Vedic Astrology isn't only concerned with predicting wealth and prosperity, it's additionally, it is about getting a better understanding of your relationship to money. Through analyzing one's chart of birth, Vedic astrologers can identify the patterns of thought or structures that could make it difficult to grow financially. Self-awareness helps people be aware of their efforts to overcome all financial hurdles and bring prosperity to their lives.

In the end In conclusion, In conclusion, Vedic Astrology is an effective instrument for understanding and increasing your financial security. When you study the theories and practices of Vedic Astrology people can get invaluable insight into their potential financials as well as make better decisions and over come any obstacle which could slow their progress in financial matters. If you're a believer in astrology or skeptical the concept of the Vedic Astrology could provide an unique view of financial planning, and assist you in unlocking the secrets of financial success.

The Role of Astrology in Financial Prosperity

Astrology is a fundamental aspect of our civilization throughout the ages. Its significant impact on many areas of life, such as finances, can't be undervalued. In this section that we'll explore the mysterious realm of Vedic Astrology, and investigate the role it plays in revealing secret to wealth and prosperity.

Vedic Astrology is a vast old system which was first discovered in India hundreds of years back. It provides profound insight into the potential of one's finances and potential opportunities ahead. When we understand the energy of cosmic rays and their impact in our personal lives it is possible to make educated decisions and take steps that are in line with our financial objectives.

One of the most important features of Vedic Astrology is the notion of "Dhana Yoga," which is a reference to the planetary patterns within a birth chart which suggest economic success. Through analyzing these patterns Astrologers can determine the possibilities of riches and best times for cash-flow gains. The knowledge gained from this analysis allows people to get the most out of the opportunities available and improve the financial results they achieve.

Furthermore, Vedic astrology provides invaluable advice on managing risks to your finances as well as making smart investment choices. Every planet has its own impact on various areas of wealth creation as well as stability in the financial realm. When they understand these influences people can adjust their financial strategies to the planets' energies and increase their odds of being successful.

In addition, astrology plays an vital role in determining the most ideal times for launching businesses or making changes to your career or even for negotiating contracts. The alignment of the planets at an exact time could significantly influence the outcomes of these projects. Through consulting an Vedic Astrologer, one will be able to identify when the best time to begin business ventures that require financial capital, and increase the likelihood of achieving success.

It's important to remember it is important to note that Vedic theology of astrology isn't magical wand that can guarantee the financial future of a person in a matter of minutes. It serves instead as an aid to individuals to make informed choices to harness the power of cosmic energy and overcome obstacles more efficiently.

Chapter 2: Basics Of Vedic Astrology

History and Origins of Vedic Astrology

Vedic Astrology Also called Jyotish, is an old Indian method of astrology which has roots deep within the rich culture of India. With a history that spans many thousands of years and spanning thousands of years, Vedic Astrology is believed to originate from the Vedas, which are the holy texts that were written by the ancient Indian wisdom.

The earliest Vedic roots of Astrology are traceable to the early religious rishis (seers) as well as sages from India with a profound understanding about the energies of the universe and their effect on the human condition. The ancient scholars carefully observed the celestial bodies as well as their movements and correlated their movements to various aspects of our lives.

The Vedas are an extensive body of information covering a variety of subjects, including Astronomy and astrology are the basis for Vedic Astrology. The Rigveda which is one of the oldest Vedas, outlines the significance of astrology as well as its relationship to cosmic forces that influence our life.

Vedic Astrology is a belief that the location of the planets during the time the person's birth date can provide useful information about their character traits as well as relationships, careers and even financial fortunes. The belief is that every planet's position and placement within the birth chart have an impact on various areas of one's life.

Through the ages the through the ages, Astrology has changed and grown and incorporated various astrological practices and methods. The oldest texts, like the Brihat Parashara Hora and the Jaimini Sutras, have provided precise guidelines and techniques for interpreting the birth chart, and also make predictions.

Recently the Vedic Astrology has been gaining recognition all over the world because of its precision and comprehensive strategy. It's not just used to guide individuals, but is also used to aid in financial planning and wealth building. The Vedic principles Astrology will provide useful insights on investment possibilities, when to make financial decisions, as well as understanding the most favorable times to grow your finances.

The understanding of the origins and story in Vedic Astrology is crucial for all looking to explore its possibilities to increase wealth and prosperity. Through a deep dive into the old wisdom and the timeless concepts of this ancient art it is possible to unlock the secrets of the art and harness energy of the universe to bring prosperity and financial success throughout their lives.

If you're a believer in astrology or just curious about the vast knowledge and insight of Vedic Astrology can provide, exploring its origins and history can be an exciting trip. It offers a wide range of possibilities, and offers a greater comprehension of the relationship between celestial bodies as well as our financial destiny.

The next chapters in "Unlocking the Secrets of Vedic Astrology: A Guide to Financial Prosperity," we explore practical uses of Vedic Astrology in the realm of financial planning. We will look at what the birth chart may provide insight on one's strengths and weak points, as well as the most favorable times to accumulate wealth, as well as strategies for boosting financial success using astrological concepts.

Begin this fascinating trip to unravel the mystery that lie behind Vedic Astrology and equip ourselves with the information to tap into the financial potential within us.

The Fundamentals of Vedic Astrology

Vedic Astrology is an ancient form of divination used throughout India for a long time. It's a potent instrument for understanding the impact of celestial bodies upon human daily life as well as for forecasting future things to come. In this section we'll explore the basics that are part of Vedic Astrology and examine how you can use it for enhancing financial wealth.

In its essence, Vedic Astrology is founded on the premise that places and positions of celestial bodies have an impact on different aspects of life which includes financial matters. When reviewing the birth chart or horoscope of a person the astrologers are able to gain insight about their financial capabilities as well as make predictions regarding the future of their finances.

The birth chart represents a visual representation of the sky at time the individual's birth. It also shows the position of the planets and their relationships to each with each other. Every planet symbolizes various aspects of our lives, and their positions in certain homes in the chart of birth can provide useful information on one's financial strengths as well as weak points.

As an example for instance, the planet Jupiter is believed to be associated with prosperity and wealth. The position of Jupiter within the birth chart could suggest the possibility of the financial future and a prosperous life. In the same way, the planet Saturn is well-known for its impact on discipline and perseverance. Its position within the birth chart could show the person's attitude to finances and the ability to accumulate and save money.

Apart from the planets in addition to the solar system, in addition to the planets, Vedic Astrology is also a study of the impact of various other aspects, including the lunar nodes, also known in the form of Rahu and Ketu as well as the rising or ascendant sign. These aspects further improve the knowledge of a person's potential for financial success and the time of opportunities in financial markets.

Knowing the basics of Vedic Astrology allows individuals to make better financial choices and make the most of favorable planet places.

Through aligning their activities with the cosmic energy, people will be able to maximise their wealth and create prosperity in their lives.

In the next sections of the guide, we'll explore different strategies and techniques to discover the secrets of Vedic Astrology to ensure financial abundance. No matter if you're new or already have a basic understanding of Vedic Astrology This guide will provide you with the necessary tools and knowledge to help you explore the realm of finance and create abundance in your personal life.

Be aware that Vedic Astrology does not promise of financial prosperity it is more of a tool for self-awareness, and making educated decision-making. If you are able to understand the basics of Vedic Astrology it will help you gain an comprehension of your finances and help you build an enlightened future.

Chapter 3: Principles Of Financial Prosperity In Vedic Astrology

Wealth and Abundance in Vedic Astrology

Vedic astrology, a long-standing Indian system of astrology provides profound insight into many aspects of our lives, such as wealth and prosperity in the financial realm. This chapter aims to unravel the secrets to prosperity and wealth by examining Vedic Astrology, offering advice and insight to those who is interested in harnessing the potential of this mysterious science to achieve successful financial growth.

In Vedic astrology, the placement and alignment of planets within the chart of birth have a significant role to play in determining an individual's financial future. When studying the planetary influence people can get an comprehension of their own financial capacity and open the gates to wealth.

One of the main aspects of Vedic Astrology that affects prosperity is that of the 2nd house called the house of finances. The house of finance represents accumulation of wealth assets, financial stability. Through analyzing the placement of planets within this house as well as their influences, astrologers may provide important insight into one's future financial outlook. A strong and favorable position in the second house of Jupiter within the 2nd house typically believed to be a sign of prosperity in the financial realm.

In addition, Vedic astrology emphasizes the importance of the ninth house which is also referred to as the"house of fortune. This house symbolizes luck, luck, and education. The favorable planetary alignments within this house could suggest opportunities for growth as well as prosperity. Beneficial aspects from Jupiter or Venus on the ninth house could increase your chances of financial success.

Furthermore, Vedic astrology recognizes the significance of certain practices or combinations of planets which have a significant impact on one's financial wellbeing. Like, for instance it is it is believed that the Dhana Yoga, created by the association of the fifth, second nineteenth and eleventh houses, is a sign of the potential to create wealth. When they are aware of and comprehend the yogas involved, people are able to harness their energy and increase wealth and abundance in their lives.

It is crucial to remember it is important to note that Vedic Astrology isn't a fixed system however it can provide insight and advice on possible chances and problems. When one is aware of their birth chart as well as the influences of the planets at playing, people can make an informed decision and take essential actions necessary to improve the financial potential of their lives.

To conclude, Vedic astrology provides a complete framework to understand the relationship between wealth and the abundance. Through studying the ninth and second houses, along with the most important yogas, people will gain insight on their wealth potential. This chapter is designed to assist anyone interested in the interplay of Vedic Astrology and Finance by guiding them down the path to uncovering the secrets of wealth and prosperity.

Recognizing Financial Opportunities via Planetary Alignments

In the field of Vedic Astrology The cosmic jig of the planets is of immense significance, not only for comprehending our individual lives but also for unlocking the secrets to wealth and prosperity. The Vedic wisdom from the past Astrology gives us an unique view of the interconnectedness of celestial bodies and the influence they exert on our opportunities in the financial realm.

The alignment of the planets at time and time when we are born establishes an ethereal blueprint for every aspect of our life as well as our financial outlook. If we can understand the intricacies of alignments between planets to gain insight into the investment opportunities we have in the future.

One of the most important concepts in the Vedic system of Astrology is the idea of Dashas and Dashas are the planetary times that control the various areas of life such as financial matters. By conducting a thorough study of these planetary times it is possible to identify ones that lead for financial prosperity and growth. When we align our decisions and actions with the energies of cosmic energy in these times and maximizing our potential for financial success.

In addition, the interaction among the planets that are in the birth chart of ours can indicate certain financial tendencies and skills. As an example, the location of Venus as the planet that is which is associated with wealth and luxurious could indicate our inherent attraction to financial issues and our capacity to draw prosperity. If we are aware of the planetary influence and influencing factors, we are able to harness the strengths of our nature and make well-informed decisions regarding our financial endeavors.

Additionally In addition, Vedic Astrology can be a valuable guideline when it comes to identifying the best times to engage in investment and financial ventures. The motion of the planets in various zodiac signs generates distinct energies that could aid or derail the financial goals of our clients. Utilizing this understanding and understanding, we can determine our commercial ventures, as well as other financial choices to be aligned with the positive cosmic energy.

Chapter 4: Analyzing The Birth Chart For Financial Success

The Importance of the Ascendant

Within the wide-ranging world of Vedic Astrology, one factor which is of great importance is the ascendant or rising sign. Sometimes referred to as"the "mask" that we wear as the ascendant, it has a significant role to play in shaping our character as well as determining how we look as well as setting the scene to ensure our financial security. The importance of understanding the ascendant is crucial for those who want to discover the mysteries of Vedic Astrology and attain prosperity in the field of finance.

The ascendant is a Zodiac sign which was ascending in the east in the time that an individual was born. It is a reflection of the person's external behaviors, how they interact with others, and their first impression upon the world around them. As a mask may conceal or expose our real self, the ascendant provides insight into our image in the eyes of others and how we portray ourselves when it comes to financial issues.

In the realm of money The ascendant has a lot of influence. It can influence our natural dispositions as well as our talents and capabilities and, in turn, affects the financial capacity of us. If, for instance, someone is born with the Taurus ascendant is likely to be a fervent entrepreneur, patient as well as a natural attraction with the physical world. This could lead to the prosperity in the financial realm, in the event that they use these talents successfully.

In addition, the ascendant affects our ability to make decisions that are essential when it comes to finance. It will determine the amount of confidence and self-confidence you have in regards to risk-taking or investment decisions. In the case of an example, someone who has an ascendant of Leo ascendant could be naturally inclined to making risky decisions, whereas a person who has an Virgo ascendant might tend to be more prudent and thoughtful.

The importance of understanding ascendant is a great way to take informed decisions when it comes to their financial situation. When identifying the ascendant of their birth and analyzing its traits you can gain insight on their strengths and weak points. The knowledge gained will allow individuals to leverage their strengths while strengthening their weaknesses, eventually leading to financial success.

As a conclusion, the ascendant is one of the most important aspects of Vedic Astrology, especially when it comes to the financial abundance. It determines our character and influences our inherent capabilities and talents and influences our ability to make informed decisions. When we recognize the importance to the ascendant people will be able to discover the secret of Vedic Astrology and tap into its potential to gain successful financial results. If you're a believer in astrology, or just intrigued by its power understanding the importance of the ascendant will provide useful insight into your finances.

Examining the Wealth Houses in the Birth Chart

The fascinating world of Vedic Astrology The birth chart acts as a compass for one's life and provides the individual's unique cosmic blueprint. A major and interesting aspect of this ancient knowledge is the capacity to uncover the mystery of prosperity and wealth. Through examining the wealth houses of your birth chart we are able to discover a lot of information about the potential of a person's wealth and success in the financial realm.

The birth chart is comprised of twelve houses that represent diverse aspects of life. Within these twelve houses, the first, sixth and eleventh provide valuable information about a person's financial health. We will look at each of them and discover their relevance in unravelling the mysteries of wealth and prosperity.

The second house, also known in the tradition of Dhana Bhava is the residence of possessions and wealth. It represents an individual's accumulation of money, assets of the material kind, as well as financial security. The power and position of the planets that reside in the house provide insight into the capacity of an individual to accumulate wealth and keep it.

In the sixth house, also known as the Upachaya Bhava This house symbolizes loans, debts and financial obligations. Though it could seem contradictory that there are negative planets in this area can provide potential opportunities to grow your finances. The challenges that come with it can motivate people to work hard and conquer obstacles. This can lead to financial wealth.

The eleventh house, also known as Labha Bhava, is considered to be the house of gains and earnings. The house is where you earn income from a variety of sources, such as investment, ventures in business as well as partnership. An eleventh house that is strong can signal a constant stream of wealth as well as the possibility of unexpected cash-flows.

The interplay of these wealth-building houses and the positions of planets in their spheres is vital to determining the financial capacity of an individual. Certain aspects like conjunctions, aspects and the planet's dignity enhance this knowledge and provide an overall picture of your financial future.

It's important to remember that although birth charts provide valuable information, it cannot define one's financial fate. the choices, actions and the mindset of each person have a major impact on the direction of their financial destiny. Through harnessing the powers of Vedic Astrology and linking our actions to the energy of the universe, we are able to unleash our full potential to wealth and prosperity.

Chapter 5: Planetary Influences On Financial Prosperity The Role Of Jupiter In Wealth Accumulation

In the world of Vedic astrology, the location and impact of planets play an important role in the direction of one's financial future. In the constellation of celestial bodies Jupiter is a prominent figure in terms of the accumulation of wealth. It is known as the planet of abundance, expansion, and knowledge, Jupiter has a profound influence on our financial well-being.

Jupiter is also known as Brihaspati and is associated with luck, development as well as success. The position of Jupiter in the birth chart will decide the amount of wealth that a person can experience through their lifetime. If Jupiter is stable and well-placed Jupiter bestows blessings which result in financial prosperity as well as prosperity.

One of the most important way that Jupiter influence the growth of wealth is the association with wisdom and knowledge.

Jupiter is considered to be the guru of the gods and is a symbol for the higher levels of education, philosophy as well as spirituality. People who have a high Jupiter tend to learning and gaining wisdom that leads to lucrative possibilities as well as financial success.

Furthermore, Jupiter governs our ability to choose wise investments and also take risk-taking with a calculated approach. Jupiter's influence can help individuals make informed financial choices which can lead to a an accumulation of wealth that lasts for a long time. Jupiter's influence encourages people to consider the big picture, broaden their perspective, and accept possibilities that are likely to yield substantial gains in financial terms.

The location of Jupiter's birth chart can also affect the financial capacity and luck of a person. If Jupiter is in a house that is favorable that could signal the natural ability for creating wealth and financial management. These people are more likely to enjoy abundance without difficulty and have financial security throughout their lifetime.

But, it's important to keep in mind that Jupiter's influence on the planet alone does not assure financial stability. Other aspects like the general strength of the birth chart planets, and personal efforts also play a crucial role. Jupiter serves as facilitator by increasing the likelihood of accumulating wealth and making sure that chances are readily available.

To tap into the power that comes from Jupiter people can engage in particular remedies and exercises. They can include observing Jupiter-related rituals, wearing stones that are associated with Jupiter or singing mantras that are dedicated to Jupiter. Talking with the help of a Vedic Astrologer with a specialization in financial matters can provide specific insights and advice for maximising Jupiter's influence on the accumulation of wealth.

In the end, Jupiter's part in the accumulation of wealth is a key factor in Vedic theology of astrology. The energy of Jupiter empowers people with knowledge, wisdom as well as the capacity to make sound financial choices. Through understanding and harnessing Jupiter's power, people will be able to discover the secret of wealth and prosperity in their finances. They can also pave the route to success and abundance.

The Impact of Venus on Financial Stability

Within the field of Vedic Astrology, celestial bodies play a major impact on many areas of life which includes our financial health. Venus is known as the goddess of love, beauty and prosperity, has vital roles in determining the stability of our finances.

Venus is also called Shukra in Vedic Astrology, is a symbol of the material world, wealth and abundance. Her position within the chart of birth could provide useful information about a person's financial capacity and potential to gain money. Venus' influence Venus may either boost the stability of financial assets, or deter it dependent on the position it is in and its interactions in conjunction with other planets.

If Venus is strong and well-positioned and well-placed, it showers blessings to the person providing financial stability and prosperity. People with these traits usually have an instinctive ability to attract prosperity and comforts. They possess a keen sense of potential financial rewards and are skilled in making smart investment choices. Furthermore, their ability influence others is often the basis for profitable business relationships and economic gains.

Contrarily the opposite, an imbalanced or weak Venus may pose problems for financial stability. These individuals might have difficulties when it comes to accumulating wealth, and may struggle to ensure financial stability. It is possible that they will experience financial turbulence and unexpected costs, as well as the absence of a stable source of income. In addition the weak Venus could indicate a tendency toward indulgence or overspending and is why it's important for people to be cautious and be disciplined in their finance matters.

Knowing the influence of Venus in relation to financial stability could help individuals make more informed choices regarding their finances. When studying the placement and the aspects of Venus in their birth charts people can gain insight about their own financial strengths as well as weakness. The knowledge gained can assist individuals in harnessing the strengths they have to increase the financial benefits and avoiding potential difficulties.

In addition, Vedic astrology offers remedies that help strengthen Venus and ease financial difficulties. This can be done by the wearing of gemstones that are associated with Venus or performing particular rituals, or participating in charitable activities. When one aligns themselves to the energy of Venus people can improve their finances and increase peace and stability.

It is vital to realize that even though Vedic Astrology can provide valuable advice however, financial stability is dependent on external factors including economic trends or personal preferences, as well as effort. Thus, it is crucial to incorporate astrological knowledge along with practical financial planning, and a systematic method to ensure long-term financial stability.

To sum up, Venus, the planet of abundance, can have an impact on the stability of finances in Vedic Astrology. The placement of Venus and its aspects within the birth chart may indicate individuals' financial capacity and the capacity they have to create riches. When they understand these influences, and following the recommended remedies to harness the energy of Venus and open the way towards financial success.

Chapter 6: Identifying Favorable Time Periods For Financial Growth

The Significance of Dashas and Bhuktis in Vedic Astrology

Within the field of Vedic and astrology, concepts of bhuktis and dashas have an immense importance. The techniques used in ancient astrology were used for centuries to discover the secret of our lives, which includes wealth and prosperity in the realm of finance. The power of the Bhuktis and dashas can provide important insights to navigate the maze of vedic financial astrology.

Dashas are a reference to the planetary cycles which influence different aspects of our life. The duration of these periods, which could vary from a few months or even years can be determined by the location of the moon during the time of the birth of our child. Every person experiences their own unique series of dashas and it's during these times the planets of certain planets have a dominating influences on our lives.

The effect of the dashas on our financial wellbeing can be profound. In the case of example, if one is going through an era dominated by the planetary Jupiter which is also known by the name of Guru dasha, they're likely to see financial growth and prosper. Jupiter is connected to wisdom, expansion and prosperity, which makes it an excellent planet-related influence to achieve successful financial growth.

Bhuktis however, on the other hand, is parts of the dasha. The shorter durations, usually lasting from a few months up or a whole year, also improve the effect of the planet that is dominant. Bhuktis could either increase or reduce the effect of the dasha depending on the planet's alignment.

The understanding of the interaction between the two can be crucial to optimize the financial outlook of a person. Through analyzing the planet's positions as well as their associated the bhuktis and dashas, vedic Astrologers are able to accurately forecast profitable times for financial gain. The knowledge gained allows individuals to make educated decisions about careers, investments and ventures in business.

Additionally, dashas and bhuktis provide information about the possible challenges or issues that could be encountered during particular times. When they know the challenges ahead of time, the beginning, one can make proactive steps to minimize risks and guarantee security in their finances.

In the end Dashas and bhuktis can be described as important tools to use in vedic financial astrology. The planetary cycles provide a profound insight into one's finances and help people achieve wealth and prosperity. In figuring out the complicated interactions between planets as well as dashas and bhuktis people can gain access to the mysteries of vedic theology, and use the power of it to gain prosperity in the field of finance.

Timing Financial Decisions for Optimal Results

When it comes to wealth and prosperity, taking the appropriate decisions at the right time could significantly influence the financial performance of our company. Vedic theology, a renowned method that integrates an understanding of the astrology with Hindu philosophical thought, provides important insights into the timing of the right financial decision to achieve optimal outcomes. Through understanding the influence of cosmic forces in our financial activities and our financial decisions, we are able to align our choices with favorable positions of the planets to bring prosperity and riches.

Vedic astrology holds that the movement and position of celestial bodies can have significant impact on all things in our life such as the financial situation. As the moon influences the tides, cosmic energy can impact our financial outcomes. When we study the chart of our birth that maps the position of planets around the time of our birth, we are able to learn more about our own financial capabilities and pinpoint the most favorable time frames for financial decision-making.

One of the fundamental ideas in making financial decisions when timing is crucial is the notion of "Muhurtha," which refers to selecting a suitable time to begin a crucial task. Vedic astrology offers guidelines to determine the most favorable muhurthas the financial sector, such as the start of the business of a brand new company and investing in stocks purchasing a property, and even taking important financial decisions.

The position of the planets within our birth chart as well as their movements can signal periods of growth in financial resources and also risks. As an example, if the planet Jupiter is often referred to as"the planet of wealth occurs in favorable positions this could signal an opportunity for financial growth as well as growth. It is also important to stay alert during solar transits which may signal the possibility of financial difficulties.

If we understand these influences of the planet that we have, we can make more informed decision-making regarding financial matters. If for instance, we are in the time of a favorable planetary transit, it could be a good time to begin investing in the creation of a new business or diversify our portfolios of investment. In contrast when there are planetary storms that can be challenging It is advisable to take a cautious approach and concentrate on safeguarding the assets we already have.

But, it's important to keep in mind that Vedic Astrology isn't any guarantee for financial success. It's a useful instrument that could provide insight and direction however, your actions and effort are crucial to getting financial wealth. Making use of the wisdom of Vedic Astrology in conjunction with a practical plan for financial management and a shrewd attitude will yield the best performance in financial endeavors.

Chapter 7: Remedies And Practices For Enhancing Financial Prosperity

Gemstones and Their Effects on Wealth

The gemstones have been adored for long periods of time not just for their beautiful beauty, however also due to their spiritual and metaphysical powers. The world of Vedic Astrology, stones are thought to have special energies that influence the way we live our lives, such as our economic prosperity. This chapter aims to investigate the intricate relationship between gemstones and wealth, providing a glimpse on how precious stones could positively affect our financial wellbeing.

Based on Vedic Astrology, every planet that we have in our solar system is linked with a particular gemstone that resonates with the energy of its. They are believed to absorb the planet's energies and align them with the energy fields of our own, which in turn attract abundance and wealth to our lives. When wearing the correct gemstone, one is able to enhance the positive energy on the planet that is associated with it and improve their financial outlook.

In particular, the dazzling yellow sapphire, also referred to as Pukhraj is connected to the solar system Jupiter. Jupiter is believed to be to be the god of abundance and expansion. This makes the yellow sapphire a great gemstone to those who seek financial success and success. The gemstone is believed to bring riches, opportunities as well as good luck, aiding in making better decisions regarding financial issues.

A different prominent gem connected to prosperity is the enchanting gemstone emerald. It is connected to the solar system Mercury. Mercury is connected to business acumen and communications skills, as well as intellect. The wear of an emerald stone is believed to improve these attributes which can lead to greater the success of financial ventures such as business ventures, corporate ventures, and investment.

Additionally to these stones and other valuable stones like ruby coral, diamond and considered to have advantages in terms of financial gain when wore conformity with Vedic the principles of astrology. But, it's important to seek out a certified Vedic expert or an astrologer for the right gemstone for one's birth chart as well as the individual's personal particular circumstances.

It is important to remember that even though gemstones have significant symbolic meaning and may have connections to prosperity, they shouldn't be relied on solely for economic success. Vedic Astrology stresses the importance of perseverance, dedication and shrewd decision-making in order to be successful financially. When used together with these traits they are believed to amplify the positive energy of our lives and align with our best interests.

The bottom line is that gemstones have been long considered effective tools for creating riches and wealth in the field of Vedic

Astrology. Though their effect may vary depending on the individual but wearing the correct gemstone that is in harmony with the birth chart as well as astrological analyses is thought to boost the prospects of financial success. It is important to look at gemstones from an unbiased view, understanding that they're not magical solution but instead catalysts to bringing our focus to our goals for financial success.

Rituals and Mantras for Attracting Financial Abundance

To achieve wealth and prosperity There are many strategies and instruments that can use to draw the potential of Vedic Astrology. The rituals as well as the mantras are among the strong practices employed for ages to draw prosperity and wealth to one's life. In this chapter we'll look at the most efficient practices and mantras to assist in unravelling the secrets of Vedic Astrology, and help pave the way to wealth and prosperity.

Rituals are a crucial element in Vedic astrology since they assist bring our energies in line in harmony with the forces of nature that govern our financial health. One of these rituals is Lakshmi Puja is a celebration that is dedicated to the goddess Of Wealth Lakshmi. When performing this ritual people can ask for the favors and blessings of Lakshmi and bring prosperity in their lives. This practice includes offering prayers, lighting incense, and performing an aarti (a practice of waving light before the god). Furthermore, one can build a shrine in their home that is dedicated to Lakshmi and conduct daily puja in order to build a stronger connection with the Goddess.

In addition to the rituals and prayers, mantras can be powerful devices that allow us to channel the desires and thoughts of our hearts toward achieving financial success. The most well-known mantras to attract financial abundance includes one called the Kubera mantra. Kubera is known as the Lord of Wealth is said to provide abundant prosperity and blessings to those who sing his mantra with fervor. When chanting the Kubera mantra on a regular basis, people are able to tap into their own spiritual power and bring the blessings of financial success into their lives.

A powerful mantra to attract prosperity in the financial realm can be found in The Lakshmi Gayatri mantra. It is a prayer to goddess Lakshmi and seeks her blessings on success and wealth. Through praying in the Lakshmi Gayatri mantra with sincerity and concentration, people are able to align their energy to the divine force of wealth and prosperity, and also attract the financial prosperity they desire.

Chapter 8: Case Studies And Examples Of Financial Success Using Vedic Astrology

Real-life Stories of Individuals who Achieved Financial Prosperity

In this chapter we explore the inspirational stories of real people who have made it financially prosperous with the help and wisdom of Vedic Astrology. The stories in this chapter are testaments to the power that transforms this ancient method and be a source of inspiration for people who are looking to find their financial potential.

Meet John an entrepreneur struggling that was at the brink of bankruptcy. Despite his best efforts the success did not come He was left with a feeling of defeat. But after consulting an Vedic Astrologer, John gained invaluable information about his financial capabilities and was offered a path to financial the success. Through following the suggestions for methods and taking advantage of favorable planet alignments John was able to overcome financial obstacles and experienced exponential growth of the business. He is now an extremely successful entrepreneur and runs an incredibly successful business.

A more remarkable tale is of Sarah the single mother who was weighed down by debt and anxiety over finances. Sarah had believed for a long time that her finances weren't in her hands. But after consulting with an Vedic Astrologer, she realized her hidden talents. Through the guidance of an astrologer, Sarah gained a fresh perception of her finances and followed the recommendations for remedies which included certain rituals and gemstone suggestions. In the process, Sarah experienced a change in her outlook and was able attract fresh opportunities and pathways to economic growth. In the present, Sarah is debt-free and lives a relaxed life and a secure life for the children she has.

These stories illustrate the profound influence on the impact Vedic Astrology can have in determining a person's financial wellbeing.

Through understanding the specific planets that influence their birth chart, they are able to align their actions and choices with cosmic energy, thus increasing the chances of the financial prosperity they desire.

It's important to remember that Vedic astral astrology isn't the only way to guarantee instant prosperity. Instead, it acts as a lighthouse that helps people tap into their personal potential, and make educated choices. Through combining the wisdom of Vedic astrology, dedication to work hard, dedication, and perseverance, anybody can gain the keys to a prosperous financial life.

If you're an avid astrologer, devotee of Vedic methods, or looking for financial prosperity The real-life tales told in this section will inspire and encourage you to set off in your own path to the financial success you desire. The universe is full of endless possibilities. With the proper instructions, you will be able to get the financial success that you want.

Analyzing Charts of Famous Personalities for Financial Insights

When it comes to pursuing wealth, it's usually instructive to look at the life of those who have made it big. Through studying the charts of celebrities by looking through Vedic astrology, it is possible to discover valuable information and advice to follow in our financial endeavors. This chapter will explore the connection between Vedic financial astrology and astrology and provides a complete information for anyone who is interested in discovering the secrets to financial prosperity.

Vedic astrology, an area of the ancient Indian wisdom, gives a different perspective on the interaction between celestial bodies as well as human daily life. When analyzing birth charts the astrologers are able to gain deep insights into a person's character, patterns, and chances to be successful. When applying these insights to financial matters and we will gain more understanding of the variables which contribute to the financial success of a person.

This chapter will go over the charts of prominent personalities who have had extraordinary financial success in their careers. When we look at these charts we will be able to identify patterns, planetarium placements as well as astrological associations that led to their successes in financial matters. By conducting a thorough study, we seek to discover common patterns and methods that could apply to our financial goals.

The first chapter begins with a discussion of the fundamentals of Vedic Astrology. It will provide the foundation needed to understand later examination. The subchapter will present important concepts like house influences from the planets, planetary influences as well as yogas, which are pertinent for financial forecasts. Examining the importance of various planets to wealth creation we will explore the roles that Jupiter,

Venus, and other celestial bodies when it comes to determining the financial performance.

We will analyze chart births of famous entrepreneurs, business tycoons and people who have accumulated significant sums of money. When we look at these charts, we'll discover the combinations of planets that led to their successes in business. We'll discuss the role of positive houses, aspects and the transits that generate prosperity and stability in the financial market.

In order to ensure that the information is practical This chapter will close with a chapter dedicated to providing readers with the ability to evaluate their own birth charts to gain insights into financial matters. Through step-bystep guidance and case studies, the readers are empowered to realize the potential of their finances through the perspective of Vedic Astrology.

In the end, the chapter "Analyzing Charts of Famous Personalities for Financial Insights" is intended as a complete guide for anyone who wants to harness the potential of Vedic Astrology to attain wealth and prosperity. When studying the charts that were born to famous people and analyzing the astrological influences that led to their successes The readers will get valuable knowledge and tools that can be used to help them on their financial success.

Chapter 9: The Most Common Falsehoods and Problems with Vedic Astrology as well as FinanceDebunking myths regarding Vedic Astrology and the Wealth

Today, in a world where the pursuit of financial success is an aim for many, people frequently seek advice from a variety of sources in order to better understand their financial position. One of the sources which has grown in popularity over time is Vedic Astrology as an old Indian discipline that offers insights on various aspects of our lives such as wealth and success.

But, there are many myths and misconceptions about Vedic Astrology as well as its relation to financial wealth. In this section our goal is to dispel the myths surrounding Vedic Astrology and provide an knowledge of the ways in which Vedic Astrology is able to assist people in their quest for wealth and prosperity.

Myth 1: Astrology in Vedic form is able to promise wealth in a matter of minutes.

The reality Truth: Reality: Astrology isn't magical wand which can instantaneously bring wealth to your life. It's a method that will provide insight into your strengths, weaknesses and possibilities. It can help you recognize the best times to be in for growth in your finances, but ultimately, your decisions and effort play a significant contribution to achieving financial prosperity.

Myth 2 The Vedic Astrology is reserved for only those who are wealthy.

The truth Reality: The truth: Vedic Astrology is suitable for all regardless of situation in terms of finances. It offers valuable advice for people from every walk of life. It will help them to make educated decisions about their finances. If you're a business manager, a proprietor or student Vedic Astrology offers insight to your individual financial situation.

Myth #3 Myth #3: Vedic Astrology is only based on luck and can't be controlled.

Realities: While Vedic Astrology is a way to consider the planetary position during the time of your birth It also focuses on the idea of Karma. This suggests that our actions and choices could affect the course of our lives. Through understanding what we are good at and weak points by studying Vedic Astrology it allows us to make mindful choices to determine your financial destiny.

Myth #4 The Vedic Astrology is obsolete and insignificant today in the world of technology.

The reality The Vedic Astrology has endured over time and remains pertinent in our modern world. Its philosophies are founded upon a deep understanding of celestial bodies, and the impact they have on our lives. By gaining a new comprehension of Vedic Astrology people can use its knowledge to understand the complex financial market and take informed choices.

To conclude In conclusion, Vedic Astrology is an effective instrument which can provide important insights into one's financial situation. In debunking the myths that surround it and exposing ourselves to the enormous possibilities and direction of Vedic Astrology can provide. No matter if you're either a believer or an atheist studying the principles behind Vedic Astrology will help you gain the new perspective and make steps to financial wealth.

Overcoming Obstacles and Limitations for Financial Growth

As we strive for wealth, we frequently face a myriad of challenges and obstacles which hinder our growth. They can be overwhelming and frustrating, but through the help of Vedic Astrology, we will uncover the ways to conquer these obstacles and reaching our goals in the financial realm.

Vedic Astrology, an ancient Indian science, provides deep insight into the forces of nature that affect our lives. In understanding the positions of planets as well as their effect on our financial health We can overcome obstructions and make way for prosperity and a bright future.

One of the fundamental concepts of Vedic Astrology is the notion of Karma and the idea that the choices and actions we make have a direct impact on our current circumstances. When we study the chart of our birth an astrologer is able to identify the karmic patterns that are present and provide ways to get over the restrictions imposed by previous choices.

The initial step to overcome challenges is awareness. Vedic Astrology is a great way to discern the strengths and weaknesses of our character and help us make informed financial choices. When we understand our inherent skills and strengths, we can make sure that we align our career and investment strategies in line with our strengths increasing our chances of achievement.

Additionally, Vedic astrology provides insights on the timeframes for investments. Through studying the transits of planets and the dasa system Astrologers are able to identify the most favorable times for accumulation of wealth and growth. This information lets us make smart decisions and take advantage of opportunities when cosmic forces work in our favor.

But, it's important to remember that although Vedic Astrology can provide valuable advice however, it's not an alternative to dedication and hard work. In order to overcome challenges, it requires determination and an active approach. The universe's energy can assist our endeavors, however it's the responsibility of us to take conscious decisions.

Apart from astrological cures that include gemstone suggestions as well as performing certain rituals It is essential to develop a positive outlook and adopt the disciplined way of growing your wealth. Through establishing sound financial habits like budgeting, savings and putting money into investments with care and overcoming limitations, we will be able to overcome them and build a strong foundation for prosperity over the long term.

Chapter 9: Integrating Vedic Astrology And Financial Planning

Integrating Astrological insights into Investment Strategies

Astrology has been a fundamental element of the human race throughout the ages, helping people through various aspects of life, not just financial matters. Vedic Astrology, specifically provides profound insight on financial success and could prove to be an effective tool for those who wish to improve their strategies for investing. If you're a veteran investor or are just beginning to learn about investing, taking astrological knowledge into consideration could open up new possibilities and help you achieve successful outcomes.

Vedic Astrology, often referred to as Jyotish, is a renowned Indian system of analysis that uses planets and their effects on the lives of humans. In understanding the energies of the planets and the impact they have on the financial world, you will gain an knowledge of trends in the market and be able to make better investment choices.

In this chapter that we'll look at how Vedic Astrology can be successfully integrated into investment strategies in order in order to maximise financial returns. In this chapter, we will examine the basic principles behind Vedic financial astrology, and then discuss the practical methods that could be used by anyone regardless of experience with the astrological system.

In the beginning, we'll introduce the idea of birth charts, which are also called horoscopes and the way they are employed as a basis to determine the financial capacity of an individual. When analyzing planets' position at time of one's birth and analyzing the planetary positions, it can be possible to determine the most favorable times to invest and also possible challenges that could be arising.

Additionally, we'll examine the importance of planet movements and the impact they have on the world of finance. In observing the motion of planets as well as their alignment to the chart of birth, you can determine the best time to enter or exit specific investing opportunities.

We will also examine the importance of astrological cures in alleviating problems with finances and encouraging prosperity. Vedic Astrology offers a variety of solutions, such as suggestions for gemstones or mantra recitations, as well as the practice of ritual, which may aid in aligning personal energies to the planetary influence and improve your financial wellbeing.

In this chapter in this chapter, we'll provide concrete instances and case studies that show the benefits of Vedic astrology to real-world situations of investment. If you're a fan of the stock market or a real estate investor or are simply trying to enhance your financial position This chapter will provide the required techniques to incorporate astrological insight in your investment strategies.

The Secrets to Unlocking Vedic Astrology The Guide to Financial Prosperity is extensive resource that enables people from every walk of life to take advantage of the knowledge and wisdom that comes from Vedic astrology and maximize the potential of financial growth. Incorporating astrological knowledge to your investment strategies you'll be able to find new opportunities for financial success, and prosper within the dynamic market of finance.

Balancing Intuition and Rationality in Financial Decision Making

In the current fast-paced, unpredictable financial environment, making informed decisions is more essential than ever. But the issue is how do we find an equilibrium between our logic and intuition when making financial decisions? The subchapter below will discuss how important it is to balance the two elements and examine the ways Vedic Astrology can aid in financial stability.

The intuition, commonly referred to as a feeling of gut or inner voice plays an integral role in the process of making decisions. It draws on our unconscious information and experience, allowing us to take quick decisions from a "gut feeling" or instinct. In contrast rationality focuses on logical reasoning as well as data analysis and analytical thinking. Both intuition and rationality are beneficial, achieving both is essential to make informed decision-making in the financial realm.

Vedic Astrology, a long-standing Indian method, provides valuable insight into the world of financial. In studying the positions of planets during when we were born, and the time that we were born Vedic astrology is able to provide insight into the strengths and weaknesses of our nature as well as our innate and rational capacities. The information gained from this study can help in getting financial success.

The ability to sense can aid us in spotting the opportunities available, identifying risk, and forming the right choices. In the process of developing our intuition with exercises like meditation or reflection, we will improve our capacity to discern decisions about our finances. But relying on our intuition could result in impulsive choices or misreading important data.

Rationality On the other hand allows for a systematic and rational method of financial decision-making. When we thoroughly analyze financial data as well as market trends as well as risk variables, we make well-informed choices to minimize possible losses while maximizing the gains. In the end, overreliance on reason can cause overthinking or miss opportunities.

The trick is to find the right balance between logic and intuition. When we combine intuition's wisdom with an analytical mind, we can take well-considered financial decisions. Vedic astrology will guide our awareness of and use our natural abilities while in urging us to take a more rational and analytical approach when necessary.

In the end, it is important to develop an enthralling synergy of the rational and intuition in the financial process of making decisions. When we acknowledge and embrace each aspect, we will be able to manage the complex financial world without fear and bring more happiness in our lives.

The final chapter "Balancing Intuition and Rationality in Financial Decision Making" stresses how important it is to integrate intuition and logic in order to attain financial success. Vedic theology is an excellent tool to understand and harnessing our inherent abilities that allow people to make educated as well as holistic financial decisions. If you're interested in Vedic Astrology, finance or simply want advice on making decisions, this chapter provides beneficial insights for all.

Chapter 10: Vedic Astrology The Core

We'll begin with the answer to the question: What is Astrology? Astrology is an obscure science of the relationship to the location of stars in the sky and life on the earth. Earth. Based on their astronomical position they determine the course of a person's future and their destiny.

This is why the time along with the exact location and specific time of our birth are crucialWe must know the precise location of the planets so that we know what the Universe has planned for us.

Astrology is an integral part of our lives for many decades. We know more about Chinese, Mayan, Babylon, Greek, and Western Astrology Some of you, particularly those who are from the Western world as I am, are likely to hear for the first time about Vedic Astrology.

What do you think of Vedic Astrology?

The Vedic Astrology is an Indian Astrology which is sometimes referred to Indian Astrology as well as Jyotish. Veda can mean literally

"wisdom", or "true knowledge" and Jyotish is a reference to

"science of light".

Vedic Astrology is considered to be a part of the sacred of Indian lifestyle and daily lifeAstrologers can be described as a kind of priest to them. I'm always amazed by the number of people I meet who are from India asking me to study their charts. They show you reverence, something that isn't as common in people from the Western world.

Vedic Astrology is among the oldest astrologythat is also the basis, or the origins of Greek astrology that is on the flip side is the foundation of the modern Western Astrology.

5

VEDIC ASTROLOGY EASY & SIMPLE

There are five major branches of Hindu Astrology:

Prashara Hora Shastra

Jaimini

Bhrigu Nadi Jyotish

KP Astrology

Nadi Astrology

Lal Kitab

The publication, Vedic Astrology Easy& Simple, is built upon Prashara Hora Shastra, which is one of the most renowned branches that is part of Vedic Astrology, followed by Jaimini.

The Hindu (Vedic) the culture of Hinduism, Vedic astrology is strongly associated with Ayurveda as well as Yoga. Astrologers refer to them as "sister sciences". Yoga improves your mental health; Ayurveda heals and harmonizes the physical body, as well as your

Vedic Astrology provides a map of your existence and assists you in fulfilling your karma and make it manifest in the best feasible way.

Prior to moving on in the process, it's essential for anyone who is new or that don't have any knowledge about Hindu Astrology to be aware of the key terms:

Rashi means zodiac sign

"Grahas the planets

Bhava the houses of the chart of astrology

The Nakshatras Nakshatras the lunar mansions constellations that form the zodiac signs.

Dasha, a planetary time

Lagna This is the Ascendant/ rising Sign.

The chart is called Varga charts or divisional charts we employ for Vedic Astrology as well as Dchartssuch as D9, D10 and much more.

Chapter 11: The Differences Between Vedic As Well As Western Astrology

Following our explanation of the basics of what Vedic Astrology is and what it is, let us address the most important issue that you are all pondering now What's the main difference in Vedic as well as Western astrology?

Indian Astrology and Western have a lot to share like the meaning of signs and symbols. However, there are many distinctions. In the pages to follow I'll show you some of them.

Calculation system

Vedic Astrology utilizes the Sidereal system. Western astrology employs it's Tropical system. The Sidereal system relies upon the true star's position the actual astronomical system which NASA utilizes. It's the reason this is called cosmic astrology. What's visible in the night sky, the similar is happening on Earth.

The tropical system relies upon the motion of the Sun which is the reason why some astrologers believe that Western theology of astrology is Ego based and this is the reason why the Western globe is a lot more Egofocused as it's ruled by the Sun and the Ego and personality dominates everything, and not the cosmic order and the natural world. There is huge differences between Indian cultural practices as well as Western society.

It is important to remember the fact that the Tropical system has the fixed equinox, meaning that, on the 21st March, the temperature will be zero degrees in Aries.

VEDIC ASTROLOGY EASY & SIMPLE

It means that the tropical system does not take into account the significance of one particular change of Earth's motion, an cosmic process known as Precession of the Equinox where, as a result of the movement of the Earth the point that marks an event known as the Vernal Equinox (Spring Equinox) is slowly moving backwards in the zodiac by one degree every 72 years.

It isn't easy, so we can simplify it The main thing I'm going to point out is the fact that our tropical system does not reveal the actual places of the stars that have moved in response to the Equinox's precession. So, on 21st March, when you gaze up at the sky, you'll notice that Sun isn't at the 0° mark in Aries and Aries, however because of Precession caused by the Equinox, Sun is at 6 degrees.

the degrees of Pisces.

Take a look at the images of the night sky that I captured on March 21, 2021 using the app for mobile phones "Night Sky".

It is evident that on the 21st day of March, Sun is located in the Zodiac sign of Pisces.

9

VEDIC ASTROLOGY EASY & SIMPLE

The main difference between the two systems increases by one degree each year for 72 years. The difference in this case is known as the "ayanamsha. It is now around 24 degree.

1900 22deg28'

1960 23deg40'

2000 23deg51'

2020 24deg8'

That means all of your planets and points are in Western

Astrology

Will

Move

forward

With

roughly 23 degrees or 24 degrees (depending on the date of your birth) in the event that you were born on a date like the 13th of

August in 1990, according to Vedic Astrology the sign you have is Sun sign of Cancer but not Leo:

Aries13th April 14th May

Taurus 14th May14th June

Gemini15th June16th July

Cancer 17th July16th August

Leo17th August15th September Virgo16th September 16th October Libra17th October 16th November Scorpio 17th November 15th December Sagittarius 16th December 14th January Capricorn15th January 12th February Aquarius13th February 14th March Pisces 15th March12th April

House Systems

Vedic Astrology employs the complete sign house system. That signifies that each house is only one sign. Western Astrology uses the complete sign house system as well as the system of houses that are not equally sized. In my Western chart, my second and first houses are controlled by the same zodiac sign because of the house system that is not equal.

VEDIC ASTROLOGY EASY & SIMPLE

The sign of the planets and rulership

Western Astrologers make use of all the planets of the major system, including Uranus, Neptune, and Pluto They usually assign the ruling that of Aquarius in the direction of Uranus, Pisces to Neptune as well as Scorpio in Pluto. Vedic astrologers however prefer the visible planets. Visible planets comprise all planets up to Saturn. Hindu Astrologers follow the old rulershipAquarius is the rulership of Saturn, Piscesby Jupiter and Scorpio is ruled by Mars.

In Vedic Astrology an important part, have in the role of shadow the planets Rahu as well as Ketu (In Western astrology they are called The North as well as the South Nodes of the Moon) Astrologers have been using the ghost planets, also known as Gulika or Mandi (Upagrahas) The the modern era of Vedic astrology these outer planets (Uranus, Neptune, Pluto) are generally used to make prediction of the world or for personal purposes in the event that they are connected to some of the other planets. This way, Uranus, Pluto, as well as Neptune can affect your birth chart at a greater level.

Aspects

Western Astrologers utilize a wide variety of angles like conjunction and sextile. They also use square, opposition and trine using tight orbs of 10 % or less dependent on the nature of angle. The planets are only impacted by other planets as well as the angles. Vedic Astrologers take a different strategy: each planet has an association with all planets within the same house and is in opposition to the house opposite and the planets that reside in the house. Mars, Saturn, and Jupiter additionally have particular features. Mars has a connection to with the 7th, 4th, and 8th houses, which is located in the same house as Saturn Jupiter is the 4th, 7th and 8th house from itself.

3rd, 7th, 10th position in itself. Jupiter 5th, 7th, 9th position away from itself.

11

VEDIC ASTROLOGY EASY & SIMPLE

There's a debate about the aspect that are associated with Rahu and Ketu Numerous astrologers think they are Rahu and Ketu do not have only a 7th, but a the 5th and 9th are related to each other as well.

Chapter 12: Zodiac Significations In Astrology

Main classification

Based on the following elements:

Fire signs Aries, Leo, Sagittarius

Earth Signs (in the constellations of Taurus, Virgo and Capricorn) Taurus, Virgo, Capricorn

Air signs Gemini, Libra, Aquarius

Water signsCancer, Scorpio, Pisces Fire signs are more active and more active and more active, impatient and impatient. The Earth signs are solid, productive, hardworking practical and slightly insecure. Air signs are romantic social, artistic, and academic. Signs of water are emotional, caring, intense and possessing a keen sense.

In accordance with the standard:

Movable (Cardinal) Aries, Cancer, Libra, Capricorn

Fixed Taurus, Leo, Scorpio, Aquarius

DualDual Gemini, Virgo, Sagittarius, Pisces Movable signs are more energetic and focused.

Fixed signs are durable rigid, rigid, and do not want to change.

Dual signposts are flexible and able to be changed.

Astrologers may divide indications based on their fertility indicators, as well:

Fruitful Cancer, Scorpio, Pisces

SemifruitfulTaurus, Libra, Aquarius

Semi barren Aries, Sagittarius, Capricorn

Barren Gemini, Leo, Virgo

VEDIC ASTROLOGY EASY & SIMPLE

ARIES

ARIES

Phrase

I am

Vedic name

Mesha

Element

Fire

Quality

Movable

Symbol

Ram

Gender

Male

Rulership

Mars is the ruler.

Parts of the body

The head, brain, and the body

the very thing itself

Nakshatras

Ashwini, Bharani, Kritika

Mooltrikona sign for

Mars

Exaltation sign for

Sun

Debilitation sign for

Saturn

VEDIC ASTROLOGY EASY & SIMPLE

Every zodiac sign represents the 12th house in the chart of astrology. Aries is the earliest zodiac symbol of the belt of the zodiac, therefore it's associated with general characteristics of the first house. It is evident in the chart above Aries is controlled by the most gruesome planet on the sky,

Mars So, this sign is an extremely unique and dynamic sign.

We could define Aries as

Afraid, impulsive intense, impatient, and passionate

Ambitious, competitive unflinching, an entrepreneur who is a man

A stout and controlling

Aries is associated with:

Power and speed

Sport and military soldiers, warriors, combatants as well as athletes

Restlessness

Temper and ego

Aries can be described as Aries is baby Zodiac's baby

Head, brain traumas, scars, cut surgery, injuries fighting

Mechanical and technical skills Engineers, mechanics and so on.

The people with Aries ascendant have a tendency to be pioneers. They are bold, proud they love sports and movements They are strong enthusiastic, intense, and passionate. Aries Lagna individuals have excellent abilities to lead, and they are able to be ambitious and selfsufficient. Naturally, it all is influenced by the entire birth Horoscope.

The downside that comes with Aries Lagna is the fact that they may be troubled by temper, anger, and Ego They may also struggle with marriage or having a spot they are able to call their home. The can be afflicted with scars around the body or head.

VEDIC ASTROLOGY EASY & SIMPLE

TAURUS

TAURUS

Phrase

I own

Vedic name

Vrsabha

Element

Earth

Quality

Fixed

Symbol

Bull

Gender

Female

Rulership

Venus is the ruler.

Parts of the body

Face is the front portion of the face.

head, a part of the throat

vocal cords

Nakshatras

Kritika, Rohini, Mrigrishira

Mooltrikona sign for Moon

Exaltation sign for Moon and Rahu (North Node of the Moon)

Debilitation sign for Ketu

VEDIC ASTROLOGY EASY & SIMPLE

Taurus is the 2nd zodiac sign in the belt of zodiac signs, and it's connected to the 2nd house on the zodiac chart.

Venus is the head of this sign the planet of love and beauty.

It is possible to define Taurus as

Solid and stable

Trustworthy and supportive

Beautiful and enjoying beauty in the world

Sensual, seeking safety with money, love and friendships

Tauris is closely related to:

Money, wealth and finance

Values and resources

Luxury

Security

Family, values of the family Family, values of family

Culture, poetry, art, speech, music, singing

Food and nature

Taurus Lagna individuals are gorgeous imaginative, imaginative, and possess a the softest and most gentle of nature. They are a lover of pleasures, great foods, and gorgeous expensive items. They may be extremely determined, hardworking and committed, and have great endurance and perseverance.

Negative characteristics issues with the early years of marriage. They can appear arrogant, confident materialism, and easy to be attracted.

VEDIC ASTROLOGY EASY & SIMPLE

GEMINI

GEMINI

Phrase

I've heard of it.

Vedic name

Mithuna

Element

Air

Quality	Dual
Symbol	A woman and a man
Gender	Male
Rulership	Mercury is the ruler.
Body components	Neck, shoulders, hands, upper lungs
Nakshatras	Mrigashira, Ardra, Punarvasu
Mooltrikona sign for	
Exaltation sign for	

Debilitation sign for

19

VEDIC ASTROLOGY EASY & SIMPLE

Gemini is the 3rd sign of the zodiac and is closely related to the third house. Mercury is the ruler of the sign.

The world of media and communications.

We can describe Gemini as:

Communication and curiosity

Restless

Quick

FlexibilityDon't want routines. routine

"Clever and funny"

The young and the childish

Sexual

Artistic

Gemini is associated with

Communication, media each communication channel is controlled by Gemini as well as gossip and social media

Twins, twin personality and twins

Short travel

Friends

Flirts

The arts and the artistic talents

Hands, handhand skills and talent People with Gemini Lagna are intelligent, friendly, and talkative. They're like chameleons who modify their character. They can look at things from different angles of view, but they are easily bored. They are extremely skilled in crafts, arts, as well as communication.

Negative character traits: they're being too focused and could become overwhelmed. They may have problems in the nervous system as well as the marriage. They can be freespirited.

VEDIC ASTROLOGY EASY & SIMPLE

CANCER

CANCER

Phrase

I'm feeling

Vedic name

Karka

Element

Water

Quality

Movable

Symbol

crab

Gender

Female

Rulership

Moon is the ruler.

Parts of the body

Breast, chest, lower lungs

Nakshatras

Punarvasu, Pushya, Ashlesha

Mooltrikona sign for

Exaltation sign for Jupiter

Debilitation sign for Mars

VEDIC ASTROLOGY EASY & SIMPLE

Cancer is the 4th zodiac symbol in the belt of zodiac signs and is closely connected to the 4th house. Moon reigns supreme over this sign, which is emotional. However, it's actionoriented and cardinal.

We could define Cancer as

Sensitive, warm emotional

intuitive and intuitive, and psychic

Selfless, nurturing

It is easy to be to be insulted.

Proactive

Familyfriendly and homeloving Zodiac sign Cancer is closely related to

Home and country,

The mother figure and the mother figure

Liquids, milk, as well as dairy products

Joy, happiness, and inner peace. Cancer Lagna have emotional issues, are introverted, maternal and are attached to their houses. They prefer working in their homes, as well as caring for people around them.

They are gifted with imagination and a strong sense of intuition.

The negative traits of this breed are their high sensitivity. They can be extremely emotional and that can lead to an angry feeling and can make them be angry and upset.

22

VEDIC ASTROLOGY EASY & SIMPLE

LEO

LEO

Phrase

I created

Vedic name

Simba

Element

Fire

Quality

Fixed

Symbol

lion

Gender

Male

Rulership

Sun is the ruler.

Parts of the body

Stomach, spine, heart

Nakshatras

Magha, Purva Phalguni,

Uttara Phalguni

Mooltrikona sign for

Sun

Exaltation sign for

Debilitation sign for

23

VEDIC ASTROLOGY EASY & SIMPLE

Leo represents the five zodiac astrological sign which is connected to the fifth house of the chart of birth. Sun rules the planet,, so it is a good sign. Ego and the personality of the person are important.

It is possible to define Leo as follows:

Proud to be an king or Queen.

Do you want to be the centre of attention

Leader, energetic and in charge

Artistic and creative

Goodhearted person

Leo is closely related to:

Media, art Cinema, art

Romance and love

Big families and children,

Education

The heart

Celebrities and politicians, monarchs

Mantras, past actions from life

Leo Ascendants can become famous, powerful and prosperous. They are a great leader and innovative abilities. They could be passionate about sports and entertainment or even political issues. They're trustworthy, loyal kind, and loving. They would rather be the boss of their own company.

Negative qualities include being insecure, arrogant and selfcentered. They may also have disagreements with their peers, as well.

VIRGO

VIRGO

Phrase

I'm analyzing

Vedic name

Kanya

Element

Earth

Quality

Dual

Symbol

Virgin on an inflatable boat

Gender

Female

Rulership

Mercury is the ruler.

Body components

Digestive tract, intestines

Nakshatras

Uttara Phalguni, Hasta,

Chitra

Mooltrikona sign for

Mercury

Exaltation sign for

Mercury

Debilitation sign for

Venus

VEDIC ASTROLOGY EASY & SIMPLE

Virgo is the 6th zodiac sign of the belt of zodiac which is connected to the traits of the sixth house. This is because the ruler of Virgo is intelligent Mercury which is what makes Virgo an excellent thinking person.

We can describe Virgo as:

Critical,

perfectionist,

precise,

practical,

calculative, detailedoriented,

Logical and well organized

The staff is friendly and courteous.

Clean, diligent, innocent

They're hardworking, they're never quitters. This is why they are extremely successful, also.

Excellent at resolving issues and disputes,

Social reformers fighters for the society social changes Virgo is associated with:

Health and healing

Food and eating

Serving the community and others

The process of addressing the pain of other people

Conflicts, disputes and litigation.

Repairing the issues and correcting the issues.

Life in the day and routine

Virgo on your chart is associated with paying some form of debt karmic.

The people with Virgo Lagna look beautiful, smart, analytical soft, shy and amiable. They enjoy nature and delicious foods and enjoy healing, communication and art, and learning. They are skilled with numbers and data computers. But, be aware that if you have a malevolent influence it will result in contrary. Virgo Lagna's inhabitants are calm romantic, sexually attractive, and secretive.

Negative characteristics can include sensitive, judgmental and hyperthinking. It is possible to have marital issues and a lack of confidence. stress, and anxiety.

26

VEDIC ASTROLOGY EASY & SIMPLE

LIBRA

LIBRA

Phrase

I unify

Vedic name

Tula

Element

Air

Quality

Movable

Symbol

Scale

Gender

Male

Rulership

Venus is the ruler.

Body components

Kidneys, large intestines,

the pelvic region

Nakshatras

Chitra, Swati, Vishakha

Mooltrikona sign for

Venus

Exaltation sign for

Saturn

Debilitation sign for

Sun

VEDIC ASTROLOGY EASY & SIMPLE

Libra is the seventh zodiac sign and is connected to the 7th house of nature within the chart of astrology. Venus is the chief ruler of Libra and is an artistic sign that is seeking harmony.

Libra could be defined as

Beautiful and artistic is a firm believer in beauty throughout all areas of life.

Soft, compassionate and warm

The popular Libra dominates the mass this is the 7th house that naturally rules.

Find harmony and peace

Dealmakers

Libra is closely related to:

Romance, love and passion

Love and relationship with spouses

Craft and art

Balance and harmony

Courts and Justice

Trade, market contract for business and commercial Negotiations

People's relationships and agreements between individuals generally.

Libra Ascendant is thought to be among the most favourable ascendants. Individuals with Libra Lagna are often popular and successful. They may have power in politics as well as leadership skills. They are able to excel in trade, business, or job positions within the government. They're friendly, social and artistic and honest. They are looking for beauty and truth. They may have an interest in the law.

Unfavorable traits are problems when it comes to marriage and sensitivities.

VEDIC ASTROLOGY EASY & SIMPLE

SCORPIO

SCORPIO

Phrase

I destroy

Vedic name

Vrischika

Element

Water

Quality

Fixed

Symbol

Scorpio

Gender

Female

Rulership

Mars rules the planet. Ketu is the ruler.

The coruler

Body components

Reproductive parts, groins

Nakshatras

Vishakha, Anuradha, Jyeshtha

Mooltrikona sign for

Exaltation sign for Ketu

Debilitation sign for Moon and Rahu

VEDIC ASTROLOGY EASY & SIMPLE

Scorpio is the eighth zodiac sign and is associated with the 8th and the 8th house is important. Scorpio is considered to be the most spiritual sign and can bring specific events of karmic nature into your daily life. It's ruled by fierce Mars as well as the spiritual Ketu.

We can describe Scorpio as:

Passionate and intense,

Mystical, secretive, deep

Stubborn and obsessive

Sexual, attractive, magnetic,

Violent and shocking

Scorpio is hidden, unnoticed and yet undiscovered.

Looking for the truth, and undiscovered Scorpio is connected to

Death and Rebirth

Transformation,

Power

Underground world, mafia

All that's secret, undiscovered, or beneath the earth

Deception and manipulation

Psychology, occult, mysticism, astrology

Depth

Sex

Karmic energy

Hidden wealth, taxes inheritance Scorpio Lagna People are sly, secretive sexual, determined and attractive. They are in need of excitement and enjoy the mysterious and dark world. They are able to be employed in medical fields and investigations, or police as well as finance.

Negative character traits: These people are often impulsive, vengeful or dangerous. and may have bad karma to be paid in their lives

SAGITTARIUS

SAGITTARIUS

Phrase

I'm a will be referring to this guide.

Vedic name

Dhanu

Element

Fire

Quality

Dual

Symbol

Horseman posing with bow

Gender

Male

Rulership

Jupiter is the ruler.

Body components

Buttocks, hips, and thighs

Nakshatras

Mula, Purva Ashadha,

Uttara Ashadha

Mooltrikona sign for

Jupiter

Exaltation sign for

Debilitation sign for

VEDIC ASTROLOGY EASY & SIMPLE

Sagittarius is the ninth zodiac sign and is closely associated with the traits of the 9th house. The ruler of the sign is the guru Jupiter which can make this sign positive as well as lucky.

Sagittarius can be defined as

Philosopher, guru, preacher,

Teacher

Knowledgeable and educated

Optimistic, fair and fortunate

Sagittarius is associated with:

Spirituality

Religion and belief system

Education, Higher Knowledge and theology

Wisdom

ExpansionThis signal signifies expansion of the building where it's put.

The written law and the laws of the Universe

Temples, ashrams, churches, etc.

Tourism and hotels

Traveling long distances

Chapter 13: Planets In Astrology

The planets are the following important topic we should be discussing in the process of knowing the sacred Vedic Astrology. The planets, also known as "grahas", represent a distinct part of our character that is part of us, our Self.

In Vedic Astrology We use:

Sun,

Moon,

Mercury,

Venus,

Mars,

Saturn,

Jupiter,

Rahu and KetuRahu is the North Node of the Moon in Western Astrology, and Ketu is the South Node of the Moon.

Neptune, Uranus, and Pluto are also known as outer planets typically utilized for predictions of the world as well as country horoscopes. They are also used to identify specific characteristics that a particular generation. In my experience, I've observed the increasing number of Vedic Astrologers are beginning to incorporate these planets into their routine. Astrology is changing and developing constantly. time .... It's like an ocean; new techniques and laws of astrology are being identified constantly time.

As a sailor I utilize the outer planet only when they are close to the planets of the inner solar system as an example, suppose that Pluto has a degree of 16 in Libra along with Venus that is 14 degrees. In this manner Venus is strongly in the darkness that is Pluto There could major changes, starting and ends due to love and relations.

Let's talk about the classification of planets right now.

39

VEDIC ASTROLOGY EASY & SIMPLE

The main feature

In Hindu Astrology, the planets are split into several types:

Natural Benefic as well as natural malefic. Benefic planets have favorable and positive fortunes and malefic planets do not. Malefic includes Sun that is mild malefic Saturn, Mars, Rahu and Ketu. The benefics are Venus and JupiterThey represent "the great benefics".

Moon and Mercury could be both beneficial or negative, based on their influence and the position within the chart. If Mercury is located next to Saturn Mercury will be able to have more negative characteristics more so than benefic.

Exaltation and debilitation you've seen in the tables of zodiac significations, there are two important phases of the planets:

the exalted and weakening state or condition. There are signs which make planets extremely cheerful and powerful. There are also signs that make them feel depressed, insecure, or other. Exaltation of a planet can make it extremely strong, and its characteristics increase and are magnified. The weak state of a planet renders it fragile, or its characteristics change and manifest differently.

There exist other states, including neutral, with a own symbol mooltrikona and own sign, that we'll discuss as well.

Modern times having planets that are debilitated does not necessarily mean that they're totally weak, and can cause misfortune. In the case of the debilitated Mercury won't provide you with a great memory or accounting skills, however it can help you think outside the box, which is distinct than the norm.

40

VEDIC ASTROLOGY EASY & SIMPLE

Below, we can observe the debilitation and elevation of planets as well as the degrees that indicate where those states are the most powerful.

Planet

Exalted

Debilitated

Sun

Aries (10deg)

Libra (10deg)

Moon

Taurus (3deg)

Scorpio (3deg)

Mercury

Virgo (15deg)

Pisces (15deg)

Venus

Pisces (27deg)

Virgo (27deg)

Mars

Capricorn (28deg)

Cancer (28deg)

Jupiter

Cancer (5deg)

Capricorn. (5deg)

Saturn

Libra (20deg)

Aries (20deg)

Rahu

Taurus

Scorpio

Ketu

Scorpio

Taurus

Rulership

Sun rules Leo

Moon rules Cancer. Moon controls Cancer

" Mercury is the ruler Mercury rules Gemini and Virgo

Venus is the ruler and controls Taurus and Libra

Mars is the ruler of Aries and Scorpio

Jupiter governs Sagittarius and Pisces

Saturn governs Capricorn and Aquarius

The sign of Rahu is the coruler of Aquarius However the planet that is ruling is Saturn. This is the same for Ketu as Ketu is coruler of Scorpio However, Mars remains "The king" of the zodiac sign.

41

VEDIC ASTROLOGY EASY & SIMPLE

Mooltrikona

Mooltrikona is the fundamental indication of a planet, the indication that the planet is able to feel at its home. The mooltrikona symbol can be signifying that the planet has the upper hand, and or it's the most aweinspiring sign of the planet. These are the signs of mooltrikona for every planet:

The sun is the mooltrikona. Sun Leo is known as the mooltrikona.

Moon Taurus

MercuryVirgo

Venus Libra

Mars Aries

Jupiter Sagittarius

SaturnAquarius

It is important to note that the level of the planet is crucial for the determination of the efficacy of exaltation, mooltrikona, and debilitation.

Friends for life, permanent adversaries, neutral two primary camps of permanently friendships:

Sun, Moon, Mars and Jupiter fire and water

The three planets Saturn, Mercury, and Venus Earth and air.

There are a variety of theories on what planets are neutral one another. Each course in astrology I taken told a distinct tale and, at first I got lost. I attempt to stick to the major planetary groups that are Sun, Moon, Mars and Jupiter are all friends. Saturn, Mercury, and Venus are the third group of companions.

In the end, I'll provide you with a much more comprehensive table of the planetary relationship and with time you'll understand the reasoning behind it.

42

VEDIC ASTROLOGY EASY & SIMPLE

Relationship

Planets

SuJu, SuMo, SuMa,

Mutual Friends

MaJu, MeVe, VeSa

Mutual Enemies

SuSa, SuVe

Mutual Neutral

MaVe, JuSa

SuMe, MoMa, MoJu,

FriendNeutral

MeSa

EnemyNeutral

MoVe, JuVe, MoSa, Ma

Me, MaSa, MeJu

FriendEnemy

MoMe

A trio of planets who are mutually and friendly with one another are three: the Sun, Mars, and Jupiter. Venus as well as Saturn are also mutually friendly, as is Saturn and Venus. Mercury along with Venus are also in a relationship with each other.

The mutual enemies include Sun and Saturn Sun and Saturn, as well as Sun as well as Venus.

The only mutually neutral entities The two are Mars and Venus as well as Jupiter as well as Saturn.

Friends Neutral Sun is a friend to Mercury to be a good friend however, Mercury is able to accept Sun as neutral. Sun as neutral. The same logic holds for different combinations: MoMa MeSa, MoJu.

neutral Jupiter recognizes Venus as an adversary However, Venus is able to accept Jupiter for neutral. Similar logic applies for other combinations.

Friends vs. Enemies Moon is a friend to Mercury as her friend and Mercury acknowledges Moon as a foe.

These planets will assist to help you once you've got the information to be able to read horoscopes the combination of two enemies within a home, could create problems for the house.

43

VEDIC ASTROLOGY EASY & SIMPLE

According to the positions of the planets on the natal chart specific to an individual, we could categorize the planets as acquaintances and as temporary adversaries.

When a planet orbits in the 2nd, 3rd and 12th from a different planet, it is deemed to be an indefinite friend.

If a star is placed 1st, 5th7th 7th 8th or 9th planet, it is an enemy for a short period of time.

It's a good thing that the majority of Astrology software automatically calculates all the information and it isn't necessary to calculate the calculations manually. While I was studying astrology I was required to verify all the information without software, therefore it was an extremely stressful moment.

The planets you see on your chart, based on their permanent or their temporary status, will be divided in the following categories:

Wonderful Freund

Friend

Neutral

Enemy

Great enemy

The nine levels of the planetary level of power/toughness: 1. Elevation

2Mooltrikona

3Signs of ownership

4. Great Freund

5 Friend

6 Neutral

7 Enemy

8 Great enemy

9 Debilitation

Therefore, the strongest position of all is exaltation. The most vulnerable spot is debilitation. Be aware that everything rests on the natal chart. Sometimes, the planet that is debilitated can give greater happiness at 44.

VEDIC ASTROLOGY EASY & SIMPLE

The modern world is not the world of the exalted. There are numerous instances. Albert Einstein had a debilitated Mercury however this was what made Einstein the "different thinker" that changed the course of history. A debilitated Venus can cause problems in love and relationships, but can also bring you lots of money as well (depending upon your chart and course).

Additional planetary states:

1. EclipsesThe cause for the phenomenon of eclipses are Rahu or Ketu. They are not planets in the physical sense They are just spots in the sky.

The upcoming Solar Eclipse Sun and Moon are in perfect conjunction with Rahu/Ketu for under 7 degrees.

Lunar Eclipse SunMoon opposition which is conjunct to Rahu/Ketu within 7 degree.

2. Retrograde planets in Vedic Astrology, they're thought to be powerful, but there are some karma is due to be repaid for, relating to the planet.

3. Combustion occurs when a planet is located too close to the Sun, Sun burns it and

it will problems related to the significance of this planet. Sun blocks them.

4. Gandanta is when an object is situated near the top of a water symbol around 29/30 degrees, or at the start of a fire sign at 1 degree, we refer to it gandanta that means "knot end" and it is often associated with drowning. The planet becomes weak and may cause some problems. Be cautious with oceans, seas and oceans, especially if there are several Gandanta planets.

SUN The King

Sun in Vedic astrology is known as Surya and, in the cabinet of planets, Sun is the King. Surya is the one who created everything. Without it, there would have no light, and there will be or life, on Earth.

The main meanings are:

The Soul, or the self, the identity, the persona

Fame, status the success of a professional, fame

Sun is the karaka (indicator) for the father.

Power,

ambitions,

rulership,

authority,

the government

Confidence, dignity selfesteem, health and energy

Eyes, vision, heart

Copper and gold the color of gold, and orange

Sunday

VEDIC ASTROLOGY EASY & SIMPLE

Sun is a mildly malefic sign since, as per Vedic Astrology, Surya is the one which brings humanity's soul to Earth Souls do not wish to remain in this place. In the place Sun is on your chart, this is the reason why that you were born and will also be linked with your destiny and the karma you've earned.

Every planet which is in close proximity to the Sun is burned.

If a planet's position is within 10 degrees of the Sun the planet will become ignited. Astrological software determines this on its own.

The Sun is the atmakaraka of nature which is the most natural signpost of the soul. Therefore, the sign of the house as well as the nakshatra in which Sun has in its nakshatra will be a large part of your character traits as well as the purpose you have for your life.

Sun is an ally of Moon, Mars, Jupiter and Jupiter, but is and is neutral to Mercury as well as an adversary along with Venus, Saturn, Rahu and Ketu.

Sun is the ruler of Leo as well. Leo is Sun's Mooltrikon sign as well.

Sun is elevated in Aries due to the fact that the Planet of the Ego is a lover of the zodiac signs that is associated with the Ego. The King loves to sit sitting on the King's throne. Sun is weak in Libra due to the fact that Libra is the symbol of the mass, and of all individuals and the King does not wish to join the majority of the people.

Sun is extremely powerful when it is in the 10th House and decreases in strength when it is placed in the 4th house.

Sun is the ruler of the constellations: Kritika, Uttara Phalguni, and Uttara Ashadha. These constellations will discuss in the coming chapters.

MOON The Queen

The the Vedic Astrology, Moon is called Chandra and is also the queen of the planets cabinet. In Hindu theology, Moon is the most important planet with most influence. We can therefore affirm that, the western Astrology is a Sunbased astrology, Jyotish is Moonbased astrology.

47

VEDIC ASTROLOGY EASY & SIMPLE

The main meanings are:

Females, Mothers feminine, fertility, femininity breast

Feelings, emotions, inner peace, imagination sensibility

Mind Common Sense

A moody, fluctuating and instability. A feeling of safety

Fame, recognition, masses, mass consciousness

Fortune, happiness, general wellbeing

Dairy and milk food as well as liquids and fluids inside the body

Cooking,

Nurses,

Silver and pearls,

White color

Monday

The Sun is the persona, however, how you express this depends upon the Moon sign. In Hindu Astrology, Chandra isn't just the mother figure however, it could also be or a cheater or sexual playerwhich can be linked with Vedic mythology.

The moon is lustful. Moon is the most lustrous of all no matter where Moon is located in your chart, it is the desire and lust.

Moon Phases:

Waxing Moon The waxing moon Moon shifts away from sun, forming a more rounded shape within the sky. The beneficial aspects that the moon has are rising.

Full Moon Full Moon SunFull Moon Sun Moon opposition very powerful and beneficial Moon.

The Waning Moon Waning Moon Moon is moving toward the Sun The shape of the moon decreases, and it becomes more obnoxious.

48

VEDIC ASTROLOGY EASY & SIMPLE

It is the benefactor to The Sun, Mars, and Jupiter. It does not consider Mercury, Venus, and Saturn as enemies. However, Rahu and Ketu will always be a threat to it, when they're both in the same house or face each other.

Taurus is the symbol of mooltrikona and exaltation for the MoonThe Moon is a sign of exaltation. Chandra enjoys luxury, beauty and affectionAll of which Taurus represents. Scorpio is the debilitation symbol of the Moon and it is not a fan of the dark, sadness, heavy emotional burdens, or hidden realms. Moon governs the sign of Cancer.

Moon is the ruler of the Nakshatras Rohini, Hasta, and Shravana.

MERCURY The Prince

Mercury in Hindu Astrology is known as Budha and it's the planet's Prince. cabinet. Based on the mythology of legend, Budha was a child of the shady love affair that existed between Moon as well as Jupiter's spouse Tara. The illicit romance which Chandra experienced is that Moon is a friend to Mercury as the friend of her (it is Moon's daughter) however, Mercury does not accept Moon as a foe since it's an illegal child.

Principal meanings of the word:

Communication, intellect, intelligence

Writing, speech, sketching, journalism

Teaching, education Publishing, education

Scholars, writers, books, papers,

Confidence,

The conscious mind, and the logic

Astrology and astrologers math, accountants, and the astrologers

Skills, Analytical abilities, and skills that are in handwork, 49

VEDIC ASTROLOGY EASY & SIMPLE

Business, trade and commerce

Lungs, nervous system,

Healing

Short distant traveling

Humor,

comedians,

Witty

and

The naughty

Individuals

Friends, classmates, twins,

Green emeralds

The sunset and the sunrise are controlled by Mercury.

Wednesday

Based on the legends, Mercury is a sexless planet.

Budha gets married Illa she was cursed with fifteen daysa woman and for 15 days a male. It's the reason Mercury is closely associated with bisexual and homosexual people also.

Mercury is a ally of Venus and Saturn It is also neutral to the Sun and is accepted as an adversary Mars, Jupiter, and the Moon.

Virgo and Gemini both are controlled by Mercury Gemini is ruled by Mercury Virgo is the mooltrikona as well as the sign of exaltation. Pisces is known as the sign of debilitation which is ruled by Mercury. Mercury is organized and practical as well as analytical. Pisces sign too dreamy for Budha as well.

"out of this world".

Mercury governs the Nakshatras Ashlesha, Jyeshta, and Revati.

VENUS Guru of Demons

Shukra is Shukra is the Vedic term used to describe Venus. The planetary cabinet is where Venus is known as the guru of the demons. Venus can be the one planet which can revive, and is able to resurrect after death. That's that Shukra is considered to be a threat to Jupiter as well as the Sun and the Moon.

Principal meanings of the word:

Love, romance, marriage, spouse 50

VEDIC ASTROLOGY EASY & SIMPLE

Beauty, comforts riches, luxury,

jewelry, conveyances and vehicles

The sexual passion and pleasure sexual pleasure, erotica

Reproductive system, semen, uterus

Art, music, artists, musicians, drama, fashion, fragrance, photography

Mantras, spells, religious rituals

Harmony and balance

Legacy

The spouse on a chart of a man's

Diamonds and Gems

White color

Friday

Venus is the friend and ally of Mercury and Saturn as well as neutral to Mars. Venus rules Taurus as well as Libra. Venus is elevated in Pisces due to the fact that Pisces is a signification of love that is pure and spiritual and love that isn't found anywhere else. Venus is weakened in Virgo since it isn't one being practical or resolve conflict and problems. Venus desires peace and love.

Venus governs the and nakshatras Bharani, Purva Phalguni, Purva Ashadha.

Mars The Commander in Chief In Jyotish, Mars is called Mangal. In the cabinet of planets, Mars is the commander. Mars is a firstclass malefic.

Principal meanings of the word:

Aggression, energy, violent impulsivity, aggression

Accidents, conflicts, trouble, dispute, cuts, burns

Determinement, ambition determination, ambition, motivation courageous deeds, courage, determination

VEDIC ASTROLOGY EASY & SIMPLE

Sports All kinds of athletes

Military

generals,

commanders,

soldiers,

policemen, guns, weapons, explosives

Sexual passion, sex

Medical fields: surgeons doctors, surgeons, etc.

Skills in technical and mechanicalEngineers, mechanics builders, engineers, etc.

Land property and siblings

Temper, anger argument, fights Blood, martial arts

Color: Red

Tuesday

Mangal is the ruler of Aries and Scorpio Mangal is exalted by the bold Capricorn and weak by Cancer. Mars is a soldier, and wants to go out on the front rather than at house, cooking in the manner of those of the Cancer signs.

Mars is an ally with Mars is a friend of Sun, Moon, and Jupiter but is not and is neutral towards Venus. The enemy of Saturn as well as Mercury. Together with Ketu, Mars has a particular relationship. They govern the Scorpio sign and have a lot that are in common. However it is a possibility that Mars occurs to be conjunct Ketu or Rahu in a chart, it can cause major issues in the house, and also in its meanings.

Astrologers have said that if you're an openminded person, Mars symbolizes your partner in your chart. If you're trying to find out what relationship you'll have then you must check Marshouses, signs as well as aspects and nakshatras. If you are a lesbian, it is recommended to be sure to check Venus. When it comes to love, of course it is essential to verify Venus regardless of whether you're a straight, or gay it is the karaka for the love of your life. Mars is the ruler of the nakshatras Drigrashira, Chitra and Dhanishta.

VEDIC ASTROLOGY EASY & SIMPLE

JUPITER Guru of Gods

In Hindu theology of astrology Jupiter is also referred to as Guru and, within the cabinet of planets, it's Cabinet Minister, Guru and the God of Gods.

The main meanings are:

Religion, philosophy Spirituality, faith, theology, devotion

Morals, wisdom and truth.

Wealth, money Prosperity, wealth

Luck, opportunity, fortune, optimism

Children

Longdistance traveling, foreign lands, foreigners, pilgrimages

"Charity and empathy

Meditation, astrology, and astrology

The husband on the chart of a woman's birth

Expansion

Legal framework, solution to issues

Gurus, teachers, bankers, priests and judges strategists

Higher level of knowledge

Color Yellow

Thursday

Guru has a positive connection with the King the Queen and the Commanderin chief in the cabinet of planetsSun, Moon, and Mars. The Guru of the Gods is the foe to the Guru of Demons, Venus, and the Guru of Gods is neutral to Saturn. Jupiter does not like Mercury, the Prince of the Cabinet, Mercury, because Jupiter is the symbol of higher understanding and law, while the Prince is a symbol of fun, laughter and flirting, as well as gossip as well as normal "low communication".

53

VEDIC ASTROLOGY EASY & SIMPLE

Jupiter is a universe that extends all that it touches.

It governs Sagittarius and Pisces as well as Pisces. Sagittarius is its primary Zodiac sign and mooltrikona. It's exalted during Cancer but is weakened by Capricorn. Jupiter is a lover of the freedom of knowledge, independence as well as spirituality. It does not like the shrewd workhardplaying, statusfocused Capricorn symbol.

Jupiter is the ruler of the nakshatras Punarvasu, Vishakha, Purva Bhadrapada.

SATURN The Servant

Saturn in the Vedic Astrology is referred to as Shani. The planetary cabinet Shani is a servant to poor people.

Chapter 14: Houses In Astrology

Astrology is the study of 12 houses, and each represents different areas that we live in. In Vedic Astrology, we employ the housesign system which signifies that every house is equal and each sign has the same house. A house's dimensions is around 30 degrees.

The chart above shows North Indian chart above how the houses are placed and their location is fixed. If you're the Virgo Ascendant and you are a Virgo Ascendant, the position of your signs would appear as:

1st house Virgo1st House is a Rising sign.

2nd House 2nd house Libra

3rd house Scorpio Scorpio

4th house Sagittarius

5th House Capricorn

6th House Aquarius

7th house 7th house Pisces

8th house Aries Aries

9th house Taurus Taurus

10th house Gemini Gemini

11.11th house Cancer

12th house Leo

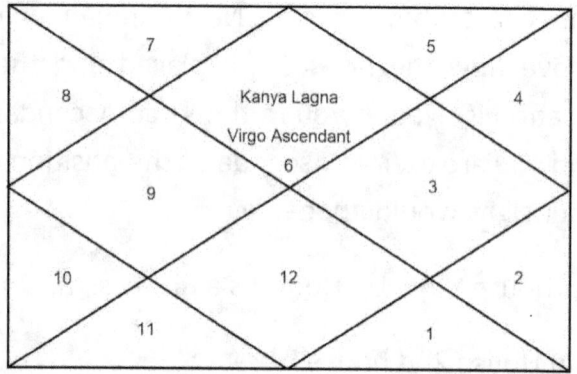

VEDIC ASTROLOGY EASY & SIMPLE

Zodiac signs may be drawn using numbers, letters or even symbols. For instance, Virgo is a good example. 6. Vi or the 12 houses are categorized into various groups.

Kendra houses

It is at the core of the horoscope chart. These 4

Houses play an important part in the human's journey The 1st house represents Self and the 4th is love and joy, while the 7th house represents love and marriage and the 10th determines the path to life and work. The houses are the biggest impact on the chart!

VEDIC ASTROLOGY EASY & SIMPLE

Trikona houses

Trikona houses fall on the 1st 5th and 9th. they are houses which bring luck and good luck. The first house includes the combination of Kendra as well as Trikona. This is why Lagna (Ascendant) can be considered to be the main house.

Dushtana homes

VEDIC ASTROLOGY EASY & SIMPLE

Dushtana houses are considered to be houses of luckthat are connected to conflict, difficulties and death. They also represent sorrow loss, suffering, and sorrow. The planets ruling the signs which are located in these homes could cause misfortunes.

Dushtana houses relate to the development of moksha, the soul and the pursuit of enlightenment. They are also connected to the spiritual and psychological aspects. The best counselors, psychologists, and spiritual leaders have their planets within the houses of dushtana.

The Third House and the Eleventh house are considered to be unlucky as well. This is due to the notion "Bhavat Bhavam", which literally means "house that is the home'. The house of the eleventh is located 6th from the house of 6th 12th house is 12th, and 12th from 12th, and the 3rd house is the 8th house of the 8th house.

Bhavat Bhavam is a term that is aimed at people who aren't beginners in Vedic

Astrology, but I'll provide you with some general details, so you will be able to see the influence on certain houses. such as the third house is affected by the 2nd and 8th house, as well so the meanings for the 3rd house are confused.

Bhavat Bhavam is a must for every house

Bhavat Bhavam from the 1st house is the house that was first that is counted as the 1st first house.

2. For the second house, the house that is counted starting from the second house, which is also the third house. The count starts by the building itself that is why the second house counts as 1. Number 2 is the third house.

The 3rd House indicates the work you've put in to make money.

63

VEDIC ASTROLOGY EASY & SIMPLE

The 3rd House 3rd house counts as the 3rd house. This will be the fifth house. It's time to count it all over again.

The 3rd house is the number 1. The 4th house is the number 2 the 3rd house is the fifth house. This is the reason why the 5th house draws on the spirit of the 3rd house, and that makes it a part of creativity and art, just as the 3rd.

4. For the 4th house, Bhavat Bhavam is the 7th house.

For the 5th house, Bhavat Bhavam is the 9th house, that's why the 9th house is associated with children/grandchildren, too.

The 6th house is the one that's in play, Bhavat Bhavam is the 11th house. That's for the fact that the 11th house may be a source of obstacles.

The 7th house is the one to consider. Bhavat Bhavam will be the first house.

The 8th house is Bhavat Bhavam, Bhavat Bhavam is the 3rd house.

The 9th house is the one that's in play, Bhavat Bhavam is the 5th house. The 5th house is also associated with rituals of the spiritual kind and mantras also.

The 10th house is Bhavat Bhavam, Bhavat Bhavam is the 7th house.

11. For the 11th house, Bhavat Bhavam is the 9th house.

12. For the 12th house, Bhavat Bhavam is the 11th house.

Houses 1,3 5, 7, 9 11 and 1 are Bhavat Bhavam for houses other than. They are influenced by the energies and significations of the houses.

Upachaya houses

Upachaya houses are located on 3rd 7th, 6th, 10th and 11th. They are getting better as they time. The planets that are placed inside these homes boost their power and prestige with time and can give positive outcomes.

Marka houses

65

VEDIC ASTROLOGY EASY & SIMPLE

The Marka homes are the 2nd house as well as the 7th. Marka means killer. Perhaps you're wondering how the 2nd and 7th houses have a connection to death. One answer is that which we've discussed previously the Bhavat Bhavam idea. The 7th is the 12th of the 8th house. The 8th house symbolizes longterm, and the 12th house represents loss. The second house is a marka as it's related to foods and resources. If there is no food or resources available and food, we'll be dead.

Kama homes

Kama houses are on the 3rd and 7th. 11th. They have to do with the desires we have in our lifeincluding travel, pleasure and friendships, love as well as money. With these homes they will help you understand the things that keep you satisfied!

VEDIC ASTROLOGY EASY & SIMPLE

Houses that provide wealth.

The 2nd, 9th and 11th houses are the wealthgiving houses that can give wealth. Based on their conditions and the planetary alignments it is possible to determine the level of your success and financial wealth.

Moksha homes

Moksha houses fall on the 4th, 8th and 12th. They relate to release of the soul. The planets in these houses will help you understand your spiritual journey.

VEDIC ASTROLOGY EASY & SIMPLE

If you are looking to determine the power of a home, you need to look at the sign, ruler of the sign, the planets which have been placed within the house or in its aspect as well as the ashtakavarga points the house is blessed with this is the most basic thing should be checked.

First House Ascendant

First house also known in the form of Ascendant, Rising sign, or Lagna Lagna Lagna Bhava. It's related to the primary zodiac sign Aries. It's a crucial home it is the chart's background. If you're under a negative influence on your ascendant, there could be a lot of problems as well as challenges throughout your the course of your life. Lagna is the combination of Kendra as well as Trikona House.

The main specifications are:

The chart determines the rest of your existence it is the base of the chart. This is your first step into this world and is the summation of your entire Horoscope.

VEDIC ASTROLOGY EASY & SIMPLE

Childhood

Personality, energy and appearance.

The Ego The Self selflove, dignity, confidence

Health and wellbeing overall wellbeing strength, happiness and longterm health.

How others will perceive yourself and how you project yourself to them not only fame and popularity but also status and prosperity

It is connected to your head and body.

Jupiter and Mercury possess directional power in this house. This implies that they are both strong.

The primary indicator of the home will be the Sun.

The 1st house is a good choice to help to neutralize a lot of negative positions could be in other areas of your chart.

The 1st house is by far the most crucial aspect it can determine what the ascendant nakshatra that is what determines your persona and the purpose of your life also. The Lord of the sign as well as its location play a significant function in the analysis of the chart. The planets placed in the first or the aspect of that house decide the character of your life and fate as well.

Now, let's consider this previous instance with Virgo ascendant.

VEDIC ASTROLOGY EASY & SIMPLE

The first house of the zodiac is Virgo The chart's ruler is Mercury. Mercury represents you, and is the planet with the highest importance in your chart. Mercury governs the 1st house as well as The 10th house

(Gemini) Venus rules the 2nd and 9th houses (Libra as well as Taurus)

Mars governs the 3rd and 8th houses Mars as the Virgo rising person can cause lots of issues because it governs

"bad houses" the 8th house that is Dushtana and the 3rd one and the 3rd house, which is a moderate Dushtana house.

Jupiter is the ruler of the 7th and 4th houses (Sagittarius as well as Pisces)

Saturn governs the 5th house and 6th houses (Capricorn as well as Aquarius)

Moon governs the 11th House.

Sun is the ruler of the 12th house and, therefore, the Sun can have a negative influence on you, too.

If a planet is ruling the good and bad houses such as Saturn in this case 5th and the 6th, it is more neutral. It can produce both good and bad outcomes, dependent on the location of the planet's position in your personal chart of natals.

Each ascendant has Functional Benefic as well as functional malefic planets! According to the majority of astrologers functional malefic planets are those who rule, or whose moolatrikona signs have been located in the 6th, 8th, or 12th houses.

The planets that are functionally benefic include:

They are the trikona house that is an ascendant, and don't possess their moolatrikona signs within the Dushtana house.

Some kendra lords, if they're friendly with the ascendant may also turn and benefic.

Rahu and Ketu do not belong They are both malefic influences.

In this case, I'd like to write about my experiences because there is a lot of confusion. Vedic Astrologers may have an alternative opinions on the planets that are beneficial or not and there's a lot of debate and disagreements.

What's important to you to be aware of is that all planets will be able to take the significance of the houses which govern the home that is put!

If we assume that you're Aries Ascendant. Mercury is within the 10th House in Capricorn. This implies that Mercury brings the power of the 3rd House (Gemini) as well as the sixth house (Virgo) into in the 10th House! The Mercury house will absorb the good and bad aspects from the houses! Remember this!

Here I'll give you my own personal view of the distinction of functional benefics and malefics in accordance with the Ascendant. Be aware that this information is my personal observations!

Aries Ascendant

Functional benefic Sun, Moon, Mars, Jupiter Functional malefic Mercury

Venus governs the 2nd and the 7th house. the influence of Venus is dependent upon its location within the chart of birth. Same for Saturn.

Taurus Ascendant

Functional benefic: Venus, Saturn, Sun, Mercury Functional malefic Jupiter, Moon Mars will depend on where it is within your chart.

Gemini Ascendant

Functional benefic Venus, Saturn, and Mercury Functional malefic Mars, Sun

Jupiter and Moon are influenced by their location in the birth chart.

71

Cancer Ascendant

Functional positive Moon, Mars

Functional Malefic Mercury

Saturn, Venus, and Jupiter Rule the 1 "good" and 1 "bad"

home, there could have good and bad outcomes that are based on the location that the sun and planets are in. Same for the Sun.

Leo Ascendant

Functional benefic Sun, Jupiter, Mars Malefic functionalMercury, Moon Venus, Saturn Rule the 1 "good" and 1 "bad" house. There can be both good and bad outcomes, based upon the positions of planets.

Virgo Ascendant

Functional benefic Venus and Mercury Functional malefic Sun, Moon, Mars Jupiter and Saturn depend on the position they are in within the chart.

Libra Ascendant

Functional beneficial Venus, Saturn Functional maleficJupiter Jupiter

Sun, Moon, Mercury and Marsaccording to their positions in the chartmay provide good or bad outcomes.

Scorpio Ascendant

Functional benefic Sun, Moon, Mars, Jupiter Functional maleficMercury

Saturn and Venus are dependent on their positions as well as their current state.

Sagittarius Ascendant

Functional benefic Sun, Mars, Jupiter Malefic functionVenus, Moon

Saturn and Mercuryare based on their positions and status.

72

VEDIC ASTROLOGY EASY & SIMPLE

Capricorn Ascendant

Functional benefics: Venus, Saturn, and Mercury The functional maleficsFunctional malefic Sun, Jupiter Mars and Moonare based on their positions and states.

Aquarius Ascendant

Functional benefic Venus, Saturn Functional maleficMalefic Moon,

Mars, Mercury, Sun and Jupiter are dependent on their location and the state of affairs.

Pisces Ascendant

Functional benefic: Jupiter, Moon, Mars Functional malefic Sun, Saturn, Venus MercuryIt is dependent on the position of the planet and its state.

If you've gained sufficient knowledge of significations, planets, houses, and the meanings they convey You will then be able to better understand the distinction. If you begin to analyze charts, you'll realize that none of the Hindu principles in the texts of the most renowned astrologers are 100% accurate, and the whole thing will depend on the particular chart of yours.

The Natural SignHouse Theory

When I took one of the courses in astrology that I took during my time at university, I discovered some interesting theories about Ascendants as well as the zodiac significations within the chart. This is slightly general, however when in conjunction with the definition of the individual chart provides amazing result!

We'll take Aries for example. Aries governs the 1st house, and is connected to personality and character. Also, wherever you find Aries within your chart in this particular sector it is possible to identify your own uniqueness.

VEDIC ASTROLOGY EASY & SIMPLE

If you are a Gemini Ascendant, this indicates you are in Aries is the 11th house of your chart. This means that you can discover your uniqueness in the 11th house, and its meanings. It is about following your goals, dreams making money, engaging with huge groups of individuals.

Taurus The Taurus Taurus is the second house. It's about cash and savings, which is also resources. Therefore, wherever you find the Taurus sector of your chart, it is possible to make money, and also have more value, savings and assets. If you are the Gemini Ascendant, the area controlled by Taurus is the 12th house. If you are an Gemini Rising sign, it is beneficial to move to a foreign country they can provide you with the opportunity to save money, have savings, or greater resources and it is possible to start an overseas family.

Gemini Gemini Gemini is the 3rd natural house.

Communication, art and abilities. The house in which Gemini will be in your chart is related to communication. It will require abilities, or the willingness to put in the effort and determination into what is required.

Cancer It is the most natural 4th house. In any place you've got Cancer within your charts, you'll experience continuous changes, like the tides and changes in the weather, and ups and downs. This house can provide the security of your emotions or look for security in your emotional life there.

Leo governs the 5th house that is natural. In which ever place is Leo in your chart there are aspects that are connected to the natural 5th home such as romance, love creative, the fields of new investment.

Virgois the ruler of the sixth house that is natural. If you are in the Virgo sector of your chart, it is where are karma issues that will not be free of conflict and problems, enemies, the possibility of healing, debts and more.

Libra rules the 7th house that is natural that governs marriage and partnerships. Whichever you are in the Libra section of your chart, it is what you'll want for your marriage and love, and what you'll do to fulfill your needs for love. If you're a Libra within the 10th House, it'll be essential that your spouse aid you in your work and if you're a Libra in the 9th house it is essential for your partner will inspire you with optimism, fresh ideas, assist you to improve, become a mentor and your teacher.

Scorpio is the ruler of the 8th house of nature. Scorpio is considered to be the most carmic zodiac symbol. It's controlled by Mars and Ketu.

In which Scorpio sector is, are karmic events that will occur which will require you to settle some bad past karma.

If Scorpio is located in the 4th house, you will experience the karmic experiences you experience are related to your the home, mother, or the country of origin, for instance.

Sagittarius natural 9th house. Whichever place you have Sagittarius on your chart, that is where you'll discover your teacher, your guru. If you've got an Capricorn ascendant, that signifies that Sagittarius is located in the 12th house of your chart. The person you consider your "guru" will be connected with foreign lands, or other indications for this 12th house. I've observed that those who have Sagittarius within the 12th house prefer to take classes or go to astrologers that do not come from their home country.

Capricorn Natural 10th House. In any place that is in the Capricorn area, is a chance to find promotion, status, career path and recognition.

Aquarius, the most natural 11th house. It is a different zodiac sign that is karmicit's ruled by Saturn as well as Rahu. Aquarius is a sign of the karmic sun. Aquarius sector can provide you with the opportunity to earn money, which will make your goals come true. but you'll also be rewarded with some sort of Karma.

75

VEDIC ASTROLOGY EASY & SIMPLE

Pisces is the most natural 12th house. In any place that is in located in the Pisces sector, is a search for escape or solitude, and you are lost and confused. The planets of Pisces are lost in the initial stages of their lives. If you're in the Pisces sector within the 10th house of your chart, this signifies that you are looking to escape via the work. If you are unhappy with the work you do, then you'll need a activity that allows you to escape and unwind. Difficulties finding your life path.

Second House

This second home is also known by the name Dhana Bhava. It's a house made of material as well as a Marka house. It is connected to Taurus, the zodiac's second signTaurus. Taurus.

The most important specifications of this home are:

A house that gives wealth controls values, savings, wealth possessions, wealth, and any types of wealth are available to us.

Job opportunities related to finance bank, finance, as well as banking.

Assets

76

VEDIC ASTROLOGY EASY & SIMPLE

Family, values of the family Traditions, family values

Security, Value system all things we cherish.

Speech and voice what do you say poetry, orators, poets.

The connection is to the neck, face the mouth and vocal cords.

The food you consume as well as eating patterns and other disorders are all visible in this section, too.

Childhood

Jupiter is known as the Karaka that is the planet with the soul from Dhana Bhava.

Third House

The 3rd house is also called by Vedic Astrology as Bratu Bhava. It is the Upachaya house. It is the 1st of the Kama houses, and lets claim that it's connected to certain issues and difficulties since it's 8th in the eighth house. This house is associated with the sign of the zodiac that's natural Gemini. Gemini.

77

VEDIC ASTROLOGY EASY & SIMPLE

Principal meanings of the word:

Communication, and all communicational channels

writing, journalism, TV, movies, social media, gossip.

How we interact and how we conduct study, and accumulate information.

Courage, willpower the ability to motivate, bravery and mental abilities, as well as excitement, curiosity, adventure and a fear.

Hobbies and interests

Any activity that involves the bodysuch as sports or dancers.

The younger siblings and brothers and cousins, friends or friends, or groups of individuals whom we choose not to.

Short distance traveling

Learning, school, education

The ability to express artistically theater and musical instruments, fine arts dancers, musicians, singing.

Art and Crafts made from handmaking sewing, sculpting painting.

It is about effort and the things which need our effort.

The shoulders, arms Neck, arms, lungs

The soul planet is Mars as Mars is the signifying planet for brothers and sisters in the Hindu Astrology If you are planning to own your own business it is essential to possess an enviable 3rd house.

VEDIC ASTROLOGY EASY & SIMPLE

Fourth House

This fourth home is referred to in the form of Shukha Bhava. It's a Kendra and mokshastyle house. The 4th House is one of the most crucial foundations along with the 1st, 7th and the 10th.

It's related to the fourth zodiac sign Cancer.

The main meaning is:

Home,

homeland,

environment,

security,

Fixed assets, properties like farms, land garden apartments, houses

The Place where we feel at home, warm and cozy.

Mother, the birthing womb, the heart chest, breast.

Your family you build can be observed through the 4th House

The comfort and luxury that is connected to homes, such as automobiles, boats and other forms of transport.

Happiness, peace of mind emotional wellbeing, mental wellbeing thoughts and mind patterns.

The grave

79

VEDIC ASTROLOGY EASY & SIMPLE

The three planets Moon, Venus, and Mars represent this house. Moon is the mother. Venus is the ruler of vehicles and Mars governs land.

The strength of direction is represented by Moon as well as Venus They feel strong within the 4th house.

Fifth House

The 5th House is called Putra Bhava. This is the 2nd Trikona house, and is connected to Leo.

Principal meanings of the word:

Children, particularly the first one pregnancies, births, conception

Creativity, selfexpression artistic energy as well as drawing and paintingthat's 3rd in the 3rd house 3rd house Bhavat Bhavam idea.

Film and stage shows

A romantic love story

Fun, sports and recreation, as well as relaxation, pleasure and leisure

Intelligence, education

VEDIC ASTROLOGY EASY & SIMPLE

Speculation Business Gambling cryptocurrency, bitcoin money, trading on the market

Religious rituals, spirituality and mantras, 9th house of the 9th house

Morals, generosity

King, government Politicians, kings

Astrology

Purva punya is a reward from karma of past lives

This is because the Karaka in the home is Jupiter.

Sixth House

The sixth house of Vedic Astrology is known as Satru Bhava. This is Upachaya house, and Dushtana house too.

It's related to the sixth zodiac sign of Virgo.

Principal meanings of the word:

Health, disease, and the body's activities

Food, eating habits Food preparation, restaurants, bars

Nutrition, diet, appetite

Healers and healers

81

VEDIC ASTROLOGY EASY & SIMPLE

Medical professionals like doctors, nurses

Servicerelated work that helps people, and helping society.

Chapter 16: Yogas

Yogas are the most distinctive feature in Vedic Astrology.

Yoga refers to combination. They can be a combination of houses, planets and the signs. Each horoscope has yogas. Some are considered to be beneficial, others are unfavorable. They are activated by the diehas. We will look at an example of one the wellknown and often seen yogas of Vedic Astrology:

Raja Yoga kingship combination which brings wealth, money and prosperity.or aspect between the lords (the planet that governs the Sign) from the Kendra and the Trikona house.

If, for instance, your fourth house in Virgo The five houses are Libra You can see you have Mercury as well as Venus are located in a conjunct chart (together within the same house) This means that they are creating Raja yoga.

Dhana Yogathis is an uplifting yoga. As per Vedic two houses, the 2nd and 11th house are the ones that provide money. They also include the 9th and 5th. If there exist internal connections between the lords of their houses, Dhana yoga manifests:

The Lord of the first house is aspected/conjunct to the lord from the 2nd house.

The lord of the second house is aspected or conjunct with The Lords from the 5th house or 9th or the 11th house.

The 5th Lord is conjunct or aspected by either the 11th, 9th Lord.

The 9th Lord is associated with or aspected by 11th Lord.

The relationship between the lords of 2nd house, 5th, 9th and 11th houses.

2nd Lord is located in the 11th house or, the 11th lord's house is situated in the 2nd.

Naturally, it is important to be aware of the power of the planets. Whether they're weak, or if the conjunction occurs within Dushtana houses, etc. all of it is important so that you can see the power of yoga.

Buddhati yoga Mercury in conjunction with the Sun

strong intellect (if Mercury is not combusted) Kala Sarpa yoga every planet is in between Rahu and Ketu on charts. As an example, Rahu is placed in the 10th and Ketu is in the 4th as well as all the other planets fall between the 4th and the 10th and this creates Kala Sarpa Yoga.

The practice will bring plenty of ups and downs and challenges but it is it is among the most successful people who practice this is because it can make your story individual and distinct.

Lakshmi yoga Moon is in conjunction to Marsand it brings wealth.

Vipraeet yoga the malefic planets within the Dushtana homes provide positive outcomes. If the god of the 6th/8th or 12th house is placed into the dushtana houses of another, this causes Vipraeet yoga. Any negative events that happen your way will bring blessings to your existence.

As an example, suppose you fail to catch your flight and forfeit the amount you purchased the ticket for However, the following day, you find out that the plane has crashed. The flight that you missed has helped save your life.

VEDIC ASTROLOGY EASY & SIMPLE

Pancha Mahapurusha yoga when planets are placed in their respective or elevated sign Kendra house. "Pancha"

5 means great "maha" means great, "purusha" means soul, which is why this type

of yoga is excellent. There are five types of yoga:

Puchaka yoga Mars in Kendra elevated or its own sign, can make you courageous and give you victory.

The astrological signification of Bhadra yoga Mercury is in the Kendra house, elevated or a sign of its own enhances your intelligence, and can make your life rich.

" Hamsa yoga Jupiter in Kendra high or exalted in the sign of its ownis positive as well as lucky.

Malavaya yoga Venus in Kendra elevated or her own signlucky in love can bring good results to your union.

Shasa yoga Saturn in Kendra either exalted or within its your own sign gives the user power and authority.

Parivartana yoga is when the planets swap their ruling significations. As an example, Moon is in Leo, Sun is in Cancer. Yoga makes planets powerful. However, if the swap involves an element of the Dushtana house, this could affect the planets as well as the force of the yoga.

Kartari yoga, also referred to as Scissors yoga, is when a planet is enveloped by malefics or benefics. In this case, for example, you've got Moon within the fourth house. However, within the 3rd house there is Ketu while on the 5th house, you're dealing with Saturn. The result is Kartari yoga, which will harm the Moon.

Another instance is when you've got Saturn located in your 4th, however within the 3rd you're dealing with Jupiter while on the 5th you're dealing with Venus. This creates Kartari yoga. However, in this case, the effects will be positive, and the impact from Saturn within the fourth house is more favorable than negative.

Sarpa yoga is where malefics are a part of the Kendra houses, they cause problems with life.

95

VEDIC ASTROLOGY EASY & SIMPLE

Neechabhanga yoga is a method of removing the cause of debilitation. If the planet of a debilitated one is placed in conjunction with a planet that is exalted, and the god of the House which the debilitated planet is located, is elevated and this can cancel the debilitation caused by that planet.

As an example, Mercury and Venus are connected in Pisces The Pisces constellation. Mercury is weaker in Pisces However, Venus is elevated this is what creates Neechabhanga yoga and provide the power to Mercury. However, Mercury may not fully recover however; it won't be as fragile, either.

There are many variations of the yoga practice, but during my personal training, I've confirmed that these are the most effective alternatives for removing the condition.

www.ingramcontent.com/pod-product-compliance
Lightning Source LLC
Chambersburg PA
CBHW071448080526
44587CB00014B/2031